The Apostle Paul
& WOMEN
in the
Church

DON WILLIAMS

A Division of G/L Publications
Glendale, California, U.S.A.

Scripture quotations are from the RSV of the Bible, copyrighted 1946 and 1952 by the Division of Christian Education of the NCCC, U.S.A., and used by permission.

Published by Regal Books Division, G/L Publications
Glendale, California 91209
Printed in U.S.A.

Library of Congress Catalog Card Number: 77-80331
ISBN 0-8307-0669-0

Third Printing, 1978

"Now these . . . were more noble . . . for they received the word with all eagerness, examining the scriptures daily to see if these things were so."
Acts 17:11

"While confusion reigns over many issues troubling the [Missouri] Synod, most people recognize how the ordination of women to the pastoral office violates the Word of God."

Professor Richard H. Warneck
Missouri Synod Lutheran Church
May, 1976

"I commend to you our sister Phoebe, a deacon of the church at Cenchreae, that you may receive her in the Lord as befits the saints, and help her in whatever she may require from you...."

Romans 16:1-2

"If the role of Christ were not taken by a man...it would be difficult to see in the minister the image of Christ. For Christ Himself was and remains a man."

Pope Paul VI
January, 1977

"I entreat Euodia and I entreat Syntyche to agree in the Lord... these women...have labored side by side with me in the gospel...."

Philippians 4:2-3

"What was Paul's understanding of women? - they were a bad influence on men, right?"

American Airlines Stewardess
October, 1976

"Husbands, love your wives, as Christ loved the church and gave Himself up for her...."

Ephesians 5:25

"To sexual love and marriage, Paul gives the most discouraging toleration...like Jesus, he had no sympathy for physical desire."

Will Durant
1944

"The husband should give to his wife her conjugal rights, and likewise the wife to her husband. For the wife does not rule over her own body, but the husband does; likewise the husband does not rule over his own body, but the wife does."

I Corinthians 7:3-4

CONTENTS

INTRODUCTION 11

I. A SURVEY OF CONTEMPORARY VIEWS 15

Fascinating Womanhood
The Total Woman
The Christian Family
The Feminine Mystique
All We're Meant To Be
Man as Male and Female

II. THE PAULINE EPISTLES 33

Romans 35
I Corinthians 49
II Corinthians 75
Galatians 79
Ephesians 87
Philippians 95
Colossians 99
I Thessalonians 103
I Timothy 109
II Timothy 121
Titus 125
Philemon 129

III. CONCLUSION 133

Woman's Place in God's Work
Women's Identity
Paul's Use of Women's Identity
Women in God's Hierarchy
Women in Partnership
In Conclusion
To the Church
To the World

NOTES 153

INTRODUCTION

The Biblical storm center for the woman's issue is the Apostle Paul. Maligned on the one hand, exonerated on the other, Paul himself is lost behind a barrage of claim and counter claim. "Paul is the true defender of women's fulfillment as wife and mother." "Paul liberates women from their repressive Jewish past." "Paul is a child of his times, demanding women to be veiled and silent." "Paul puts women in their place: subordinate to men." "Paul is an inconsistent rabbi in his approach to scripture." "Paul sets women free: in Christ there is neither male nor female." "Paul would never allow for women's ordination" - and on and on it goes.

The debate is heated because the issues are crucial. Questions of Biblical authority surface. How can the Bible be the word of God and Paul's "archaic" teaching on women still be inspired? Where does Paul teach us eternal truth and where is he simply responding to the needs of his own age? What in his letters is merely "cultural" and how are we to know this? If Paul is wrong at one point how can we trust him anywhere?

Questions on theology, family, and church order also surface. Is the Pauline woman essentially domestic? What is her proper role in the church? Should women teach men? Is the ordination of women a violation of God's order? What does submission mean? What does male headship mean? Needless to say, the answers given are often both varied and confusing.

The question of women is one of the crucial issues facing the church and the world today. Thus it alienates and divides serious Christians and even whole denominations. Early in January,

1977, Pope Paul VI denied women's ordination into the priesthood. *Time Magazine* headlined its article, "Pope Paul to Women: Keep Out."[1] At about the same time, Bishop Moore ordained Ellen Marie Barrett, a lesbian, to the Episcopal priesthood. No wonder the world watches the church with skepticism and confusion.

In the following study we will begin with a review of current, popular literature on women, especially as it relates to Paul. This will focus the issues for us on a broad spectrum.

Next we will turn to the Apostle's letters. Taking them one by one we will first establish the historical context in which they were written, noting major themes and issues. Then we will study each passage where women are mentioned, seeking a comprehensive picture of Paul's understanding of the woman's role theologically, historically and practically. Each text must be seen in its context, and as Augustine said, scripture must interpret scripture.

Finally we will reach our conclusions as we relate the contemporary questions to Paul's letters and discover how the Apostle both answers these questions and raises his own.

Our own position should be stated at the outset: Paul's writings are the inspired word of God. This word is addressed to concrete historical situations which must be understood for its proper interpretation. At the same time, we can presume that Paul is consistent in his understanding of women in the church both as inspired Apostle and unequaled theologian. Thus there is an underlying consistency even in the so-called "problem passages" although this may not be seen at first glance. We launch this study confident that our conclusions will bear this out. What Paul teaches is not only consistent but true and the church today desperately needs that truth.

To orient ourselves to the issues of Paul and women we shall begin by reviewing a spectrum of books which are popular today. These have been chosen because they have had wide readership -

several being "best-sellers." Their questions and conclusions have had a massive impact upon millions of people and much of what those in and out of the church think has been formed by them. While the majority are not "theological" works, they nonetheless assert or imply theological assumptions. Their contemporary style and practical application (for the most part) has aided in communication and sales.

Our survey includes the traditional views of Helen Andelin's *Fascinating Womanhood*, Marabel Morgan's *The Total Woman*, and Larry Christenson's *The Christian Family*. Then we will focus on Betty Friedan's revolutionary *The Feminine Mystique*, followed by Biblical responses from Letha Scanzoni's and Nancy Hardesty's *All We're Meant To Be* and Paul Jewett's *Man as Male and Female*.[1]

After this review we will be more in touch with major questions and issues in a contemporary setting. With the exception of Betty Friedan all our authors refer to Paul as an authority for their conclusions. Following this survey we will then engage the Pauline letters themselves.

PART
ONE

A SURVEY OF
CONTEMPORARY
VIEWS

Fascinating Womanhood

Helen Andelin calls women to find fulfillment in acquiring "celestial love" from their men. This is accomplished through a clever insight into the male ego. The message is simple. Find out what a man wants and needs, give it to him, and he will worship you forever.

For Andelin, the male lives in constant insecurity and needs a woman who will make him feel like a man. His desires are for a mother, on the one hand, who understands him, has deep inner happiness, a worthy character and who is a domestic goddess, and for a child, on the other hand, who is feminine, radiates happiness, is fresh in appearance and manner, and childlike. In other words, a man wants both a mother to protect him and a child whom he can dominate. The perfect woman will give him both - she will protect his weak manhood and make him "feel" like a man while allowing him to think he dominates her. She will be both angelic and human, mother and child.

As mother, the woman must accept her man at face value and admire his manly qualities; this builds his male pride. Andelin writes, "It is this realization of his masculinity that stirs his soul, and arouses his sentiment towards the woman who has made him feel this way."[2]

The role of the man is to be guide, protector, and provider. This expresses his burning desire to be superior over women. The fascinating woman makes him feel this way even if he isn't.[3] Thus when consulted on major decisions the woman must not give rational advice - this is masculine. She must "flounder and flutter" because it makes the man feel superior.

Furthermore, men have been created with larger muscles and greater endurance and women have always needed protection from the dangers, strenuous work and difficulties of life. Thus Andelin exhorts the ideal woman "to become the fragile dependent creature that nature intended you to be."[4] She must make her man "Number One." "He wants to be the King-pin around which all other activities of her life revolve."[5]

As mother, woman is to be a "Domestic Goddess." Her homelife is her occupation because this is what a man wants. "The faithful performance of womanly duties also brings woman inner happiness."[6]

As child, woman is to be girlish, dependent, delicate - filled with "teasing playfulness," "sauciness," with underlying trust and tenderness. This arouses the male need to protect and shelter her.

Thus the woman is to observe how children dress and act and then she is to emulate them. The woman must not be intelligent and competent (these are male characteristics). "In the presence of such strength and ability in a mere woman, he feels like a futile, ineffectual imitation of a man."[7] Thus, "You must dispense with any air of strength and ability, of competence and fearlessness and acquire instead an air of frail dependency upon man to take care of you."[8]

To insure being a fascinating woman, training should be "as wife, mother, homemaker as well as good citizen, rather than for a specific career."[9]

Andelin bases her picture of man and woman in part on biology, and in part on the Bible. The male is stronger, the female weaker. She then quotes from Genesis 3 that man should rule over woman and continues, "The Apostle Paul tells us that woman is to *'reverence'* her husband and he says, *'Submit yourselves unto your own husbands'*."[10] All of this, however, is true because of Andelin's penetrating psychology which sees the male as fearful and insecure, needing mother's love and child's "girlish dependency," which when given will create the worshipping adoration which all women seek. By 1973 Andelin's book was in its 22nd printing, eloquent witness to its success.

The Total Woman

Marabel Morgan writes out of her own experience. Because of deep personal unhappiness, she decided to change herself by applying "certain principles to my marriage."[11] From this emerged the picture of the Total Woman." Offering an appropriate teaser Morgan writes, "I do believe it is possible ...for almost any wife to have her husband absolutely adore her in just a few weeks time. She can revive romance, re-establish communication, break down barriers, and put sizzle back into her marriage. It really is up to her. She has the power."[12]

Rather than offering a definition of the Total Woman, Morgan launches into the "how to." Borrowing business tips, she proposes freedom from the "4:30 syndrome" (panic before the husband comes home) by reorganizing and doing hard things first. If time-management "works for a steel factory, it will work in your house factory."[13] The promise is then given: "When you're organized and efficient, his flame of love will begin to flicker and burn."[14]

Next, Morgan turns to "interior decorating." This is not the home; this is the Total Woman. After writing out a philosophy of life, the redecorated wife is to engage in meaningful goal setting.[15]

Now comes the Total Woman's attitude toward her husband. The key is unconditional love. "Your husband needs your acceptance ...(then) there won't be enough hours for him to spend with you. The barriers between you will just melt away."[16] This means an end to nagging. "A Total Woman caters to her man's special quirks, whether it be in salads, sex or sports. She makes his home his haven, a place to which he can run."[17]

Basic to Morgan's book is the thesis that women need to be loved while men need to be admired.[18] Thus she offers an answer to meeting these structural needs: If the wife admires her husband, he will love his wife and all will be well. Women have an implied superiority, however, because "behind every great man is a great woman, loving him and meeting his needs."[19]

Furthermore, Morgan calls upon the Total Woman to adapt to her mate. He is the ruler of the roost. "Man and woman, although equal in status, are different in function. God ordained man to be the head of the family...."[20] This does not mean that the Total Woman is a slave. As she adapts to her husband's way, "He in turn will gratefully respond by trying to make it up to her and grant her desires."[21] The man doesn't want a nagging wife or a doormat, he wants "one with dignity and opinions and spunk, but one who will leave the final decision to him."[22] Thus Morgan concludes, "It is only when a woman surrenders her life to her husband, reveres and worships him, and is willing to serve him, that she becomes really beautiful to him. She becomes a priceless jewel, the glory of femininity, his queen!"[23]

Morgan proceeds to offer advice in recovering an exciting sex life and proposes variations and attitudes to accomplish "super sex." Her theological ground is simple: "The Creator of sex intended for His creatures to enjoy it."[24]

This is then followed by calls to good communication and parenting. Morgan concludes with her own testimony about how Christ has given her the power to become a Total Woman. "God is waiting and wanting to fill your vacuum, to make you complete. Total. Right now you can become a Total Woman."[25]

What then is the Total Woman? Concluding her book, Morgan ventures some definitions. A Total Woman is a new attitude about self, husband and children. A Total Woman "starts with the premise that every woman can be made whole."[26] A Total Woman is "a warm, loving homemaker ...She is a sizzling lover ...She is a woman who inspires ...children to reach out and up."[27] "A Total Woman is a person in her own right. She has a sense of personal security and self respect."[28] The Total Woman is responsible first to God, then to her husband, then to her children, and only then to profession or public. The Total Woman finds basic fulfillment as wife and mother under God. And the Total Woman is a "Number One Best Seller" as the Pocket Book edition trumpets.

The Christian Family

Larry Christenson calls families to establish "Divine Order" in the home, which is "the relationship of order and authority between the various members in a family," and to practice the presence of Jesus.[29]

Following the lead of a 19th century German pastor, H. W. J. Thiersch,[30] Christenson would order the family according to the principle of "headship," where "each member of the family lives under the authority of the 'head' whom God has appointed."[31] Thus the wife is to live under the authority of her husband and is responsible to him for the way she manages home and family.[32] Her authority over the children is derived from him.[33]

The establishment of this order is critical for the family today. Its well-being and happiness is "absolutely dependent upon the observance of His [God's] divinely appointed order."[34]

For women, submission to the husband is necessary. Christenson defines this as yielding "humble and intelligent obedience to an ordained power or authority."[35] God means for women to be sheltered from many of the rough encounters of life. Since the woman is vulnerable physically, emotionally, psychologically and spiritually, she needs her husband's authority and protection. She is meant to be free from the "emotional burden" of representing the family to the community.[36] By subordination to her husband she is also free from the "burden" of the "authority and responsibility" of decision.[37]

Christenson admits what Andelin implies, that "God has given to women great talents and abilities. Their intelligence is equal to men. Their stamina and emotional endurance often greater."[38] Nevertheless, the divine pattern is set. Christenson exhorts, "Wives, rejoice in your husband's authority over you! Be subject to him in all things. It is your special privilege to move under the protection of his authority. It is within this pattern of Divine Order that the Lord will meet you and bless you...."[39]

Husbands, however, are called to exercise their authority "in the sacrifice of one's self."[40] This is executed by supporting the family physically: "Stronger shoulders are given to the man; he has a greater natural strength of mind to enable him to stand up under the pressure ...the heart of a woman is more easily discouraged and dejected. God has made her that way."[41]

Authority as sacrifice is also evidenced by the husband's care for his wife's spiritual welfare and by his humbling himself before her.[42]

Christenson builds most of his exposition on Paul's letter to the Ephesians, 5:21-33. For him this presupposes the opening chapters of Genesis where "There is a firm, unalterable decree of God in the position of men and women."[43]

That this book has filled a vacuum is clear from its sale of now over 800,000 copies.

The Feminine Mystique

Betty Friedan in 1963 published a book that became a turning point for woman's consciousness in the United States. Sensing frustration and emptiness among thousands of women and having a reporter's instinct, Friedan went after the story which exposed a basic loss of identity for women reduced solely to wife and mother roles. In the culture the blame for this was often attributed to a lack of sexual fulfillment, too much education and a surrender of femininity. Friedan saw the loss, however, due to embracing the all-pervasive "feminine mystique."

This mystique said that women's only commitment is to the fulfillment of her own femininity. Her problem is that she has envied man: "women tried to be like men, instead of accepting their own nature, which can find fulfillment only in sexual passivity, male domination, and nurturing maternal love."[44] Friedan comments, "When a mystique is strong, it makes its own fiction of fact."[45]

This mystique was grounded in a "mystical religion" justified by Freudian psychology which gave a scientific ground for woman's inferiority. Under the banner of "anatomy is destiny" women were determined by their "inferior" sexual structure in comparison to the male. Because of their "castration complex" women were held to be wounded in their self-love and thus never able to funtion as fully as the male.[46] Freud's definition of woman gave the conventional image of femininity new authority.[47] The new psychological religion "made a virtue of sex, removed all sin from private vice, and cast suspicion on high aspirations of the mind and spirit."[48] Women would find fulfillment (compensation) for their biological inferiority by being wives and mothers and living vicariously through their husbands and children. A woman's problems were now defined as anything that thwarts her house-wifely adjustment.

For Friedan, the problem for women is not sex but identity, "a stunting or evasion of growth that is perpetrated by the feminine mystique. It is my thesis that as the Victorian culture did not permit women to accept or gratify their basic sexual needs, our culture does not permit women to accept or gratify their needs to grow and fulfill their potentialities as human beings, a need which is not solely defined by their sexual role."[49]

The myth of the feminine mystique has been reinforced by functionalism in psychology and sociology where the goal is adjustment rather than change,[50] and sex-directed education where the goal is not to develop the self but to develop sexual functions.[51]

It has also been reinforced by the need of post-World War II Americans to find security at home, and by big business' need to sell home consumption products in a peace-time economy. "Why is it never said that the really crucial function, the really important role that women serve as housewives is *to buy more things for the house?*"[52]

While American businesses did not create the feminine mystique, "they are the most powerful of its perpetrators; it is their millions which blanket the land with persuasive images, flattering the American housewife, diverting her guilt and disguising her growing sense of emptiness."[53]

Within the mystique sex is the only frontier left for women, and it becomes increasingly a "joyless national compulsion."[54] It is "sex without self."[55]

For Friedan, women need to grow, not adjust. The unique human capacity is the ability to transcend the present, to act in light of the possible. "The only way for a woman, as for a man, to find herself, to know herself as a person, is by creative work of her own."[56] Apart from this, the frustration remains.

While Friedan does not mention the Bible or Paul directly, she asserts that "our houses and schools and churches" are built around the lie of the feminine mystique.[57] Of the early advocates for women's rights she notes, "At every step of the way, the feminists had to fight the conception that they were violating the God-given nature of woman."[58] For Friedan the culture today justifies woman's inferiority upon secular grounds just as it previously did on religious grounds.

In ten years Friedan's book has sold 2 million copies. It hit a nerve.

All We're Meant To Be

Letha Scanzoni and Nancy Hardesty respond to women's liberation by offering a Biblical approach. While admitting various attitudes in the Bible to the male-female polarity, including debarment (women segregated during their menstrual cycle), complementation, and synthesis (the unity of 'one flesh'), their ideal is "transcendency," based on Galatians 3:28, "There is neither...male nor female; for you are all one in Christ Jesus."

They assert that "Christianity has the potential of offering transcendency as the solution to the problem of suspiciousness and separation between the sexes - a transcendency made possible because men and women stand on equal footing as fellow members of the Kingdom of God. Galatians 3:28, in our opinion, holds the key to bringing harmony and removing the dissonant clash that is bound to exist as long as one sex is looked upon as superior and the other as being inferior and the source of evil."[59]

In pursuing the thesis of "transcendency," Scanzoni and Hardesty deny that God is male or female. God is the " 'Thou' in whose presence we stand at all times."[60]

The Pauline passages which seem to imply male superiority are either misinterpreted, as in the case of male headship in I Corinthians 11:3,[61] or are "traditional rabbinic understanding...."[62] Thus when Paul speaks of woman as the glory of man he uses "a rather curious rabbinic interpretation."[63] The ideal is the Trinity where the "Godhead is not a hierarchy or a pantheon of gods, but a loving union of three equal persons."[64] Thus male and female are to reflect this loving union - in "transcendence."

The Pauline materials which call for women being veiled find their essential justification in "social custom."[65] The command to women to be silent during worship in Corinth arises because "These women were interrupting the meetings with questions."[66] Thus the authors conclude, "Whatever the reason, the verses do not prohibit a ministry for women in the church but simply assert that Christian meetings should be orderly."[67]

The prohibition over women teaching men in I Timothy 2:12 reflects "a concern for maintaining the cultural status quo, for not transgressing the marital social roles."[68] Thus the only passage in

Paul's letters with normative theological weight is Galatians 3:28, "You are all one in Christ Jesus." All the rest are "concerned with practical matters."[69]

Having established this Biblical foundation Scanzoni and Hardesty turn to biology and culture. The roles of male and female "are totally determined by culture."[70] Sexual roles are stereotyped "lest our sexual identity be questioned."[71] Once we accept our basic unity, however, both male and female realize that "communication is possible only between those who are the same - that is the message of creation and the Incarnation."[72] Thus, "transcendency" is the ideal.

The equality of the sexes reveals that masculine superiority is another name for pride.[73] The pattern of husbands loving their wives as Christ loved the church works itself out toward "Egalitarianism and democracy in the home."[74] Scanzoni and Hardesty write, "To insist that marriage must be maintained as a hierarchy because otherwise the Christ-church analogy breaks down is like saying that all nations must have a monarchy because other forms of government fail to reproduce the picture of God's Kingship over all the earth."[75] The Biblical conception of marriage is a partnership, a covenant.[76] This will work itself out in mutuality in sexual relationships.[77] Women are no longer merely valued for producing male children.[78] Now motherhood is not an inevitable destiny but a free choice in response to the call of God.[79]

So too, a single life-style may be a call and gift of God. Since sexual union is not the goal of our existence, deeply meaningful relationships can exist apart from marriage.[80]

With the full acceptance of women the church will no longer waste the spiritual gifts given to them.[81] At the same time, women must be free also to work. The real question is: "Should human beings have a choice about what they will do with their lives?"[82] The choice of wife-mother or career must be given "just as men are given choices."[83] Choice is essential to the Christian life and in our society reward comes for achievement that is academic and vocational. As a wife is fulfilled in the world she may be better able to love herself and thus love her neighbor and husband and family.[84] Scanzoni and Hardesty conclude, ''We must begin to implement Galatians 3:28, to transcend the limitations our culture has placed on us because of our sex.''[85] As their book enters its second printing since 1974 they are being heard.

Man As Male and Female

In a clearly theological work, Paul Jewett proposes that man (humankind) must be understood as male and female based on Genesis 1:27, ''And God created man in His own image, in the image of God created He him; male and female created He them.''

Jewett states his thesis: ''As God is a fellowship in Himself (Trinity) so MAN is a fellowship in himself, and the fundamental form of this fellowship...is that of male and female. This view of man's being...implies a partnership in life....''[86]

In contrast to ''partnership'' the alternative Biblical view is a hierarchy where woman is subordinate and inferior to man. This model Jewett rejects, arguing from Genesis 1:27, the example of Jesus, and Paul in Galatians 3:28, that in Christ there is neither male nor female.

Following Karl Barth, Jewett sees man created in the image of God as man-in-fellowship, and the primary form of this fellowship as male and female.[87] Thus we are called to live as man *or* woman and as man *and* woman. Jewett rules out any attempt to transcend our dual sexuality in terms of an ideal humanity, ''and in affirming our own sex, we should accept and affirm the other sex as essential to our own, confessing that God has so created us that it is not good that we should be alone.''[88]

In contrast to the ''partnership'' model of male and female relationships, stands the hierarchical model. Jewett claims that,

" ...the case for hierarchy ...requires one to argue not only for the priority but also the superiority of the male."[89]

For Jewett, it is Paul who is most responsible, due to his rabbinic background, for making hierarchy the norm in the church.[90] The Apostle teaches that male headship "is a divine absolute, transcending the relativities of time and place."[91] Arguments for a "chain of command," husband to wife to children, are based in Paul's epistles.[92] From some of the Apostle's statements such as the veiling of women, their silence in the church, their submissiveness to their husbands, and their not teaching men emerges the subordination and inferiority of women.[93] All of this is not merely Paul's cultural or temporary response to the immediate needs of his churches, but it is grounded in the Apostle's rabbinic, paternalistic understanding of the Old Testament and the structure of reality as hierarchy. This determines Jewett's interpretation of all of the Pauline texts. Thus he concludes that for Paul "The subordination of the woman to the man is an essential part of the hierarchy which God Himself has established to ensure a proper order in the relationships of life."[94]

For Jewett the fact that women are different from men is not the same as women being subordinate to men. He admits, "The concept of hierarchy, to be sure, does not in itself entail superiority and inferiority, but only that some are *over*, others are *under;* some exercise authority, others submit to it."[95] But if men exercise authority over women their superiority cannot be avoided. Man created, however, as male and female is "inimical to a doctrine of sexual hierarchy," it is a "fellowship of equals under God."[96]

At one point Paul moves beyond hierarchy to partnership. This is in Galatians 3:28 where there is neither male nor female in Christ. Jewett calls this text the "Magna Carta of Humanity."[97] Here Paul is no longer a rabbi; here he is a Christian Apostle and the church must move forward to order her life from this text.[98]

Since revelation is historical and the Bible human as well as divine, we can allow for this contradiction in Paul, according to Jewett. Revelation redeems history and culture "and redemption is a process, sometimes a slow and gradual process."[99]

Needless to say Jewett's book created a storm in evangelical circles. The authority of scripture seemed compromised to some; the structure of God's order seemed destroyed by others. Still for others, the direction for the theological liberation of women seemed established.

Summary

Having surveyed a broad cross-section of recent authors, the questions are now clear. Does Paul decree that the woman's role is God-ordained to be that of wife and mother (Andelin, Morgan, Christenson)? If so, what of the increasing number of single and professional women? Are they out of God's will or missing His best?

For Paul, is God's order for the wife to be submissive to her husband, deriving all authority from him (Christenson)? If so, how can there be spiritual equality and authority for the wife directly from Christ Himself: "There is neither male nor female for you are all one in Christ Jesus" (Galatians 3:28)?

Must women be liberated from wife/mother roles today to find their own identity as persons and engage in professions to be growing people (Friedan)? If so does this mean that personhood is found in new roles, rather than in the self and especially in the self related to God?

Is the Biblical ideal the transcendence of our sexuality (Scanzoni and Hardesty)? If so, why did God create us as male and female to begin with?

Does Paul's understanding of "hierarchy" stand in conflict with the ideal of "partnership" (Jewett)? If so, on what ground may we choose one over the other?

Because of these pressing questions and the overall issue of women and their role and ministry in the church, we are driven back to Paul's letters themselves. The final questions are: "What do the texts say?" and "How are we to apply them?"

The popular procedure is to look at the "controversial passages" on woman's veiling and silence and contrast or compare them with the text of Galatians 3:28, "You are all one in Christ Jesus." Our method, however, will be different. Each of Paul's letters will be studied in its historical context with care given to *all* references to women whether they emerge from the Old Testament, or early church practice, Paul's personal relationships, or his theological treatments. A brief introduction to each letter[100] is followed by an exposition of every text referring to women. Thus we hope to achieve a substantial picture of the Apostle Paul and women in the church.

PART TWO

THE PAULINE EPISTLES

ROMANS

Introduction

Paul directs his greatest theological exposition to a church he has yet to visit (1:13). His intention is to guarantee a warm welcome, to achieve an opportunity to preach the gospel in Rome, and to secure a base for evangelism westward - eventually Spain (15:24).

The issue dogging the Apostle is whether he will be accepted by the Roman church. Paul is a man of controversy. Legalistic believers have attempted to subvert his work - is Paul really an Apostle? Does he preach the gospel faithfully? What of the Old Testament law? These are issues not easily laid to rest.

At the same time, Paul's pioneer work in the East is done. Since he will not build upon another man's foundation, he must move on (15:18-23). His eyes turn toward the capital of the Empire. How his pulse must have raced as he thought of preaching Christ within range of Nero himself.

To prepare his way to Rome and to secure his welcome there, the Apostle lays out his gospel for the church. God's wrath against man's sin: the corruption of the Gentiles and the hypocrisy of the Jews is announced (1:18ff). Then when all are helpless before divine justice, God reveals His gift of righteousness in the death of Jesus Christ for sin (3:21ff). Moreover, for the Jew His grace is seen to be consistent with what He promised to Abraham. It also undoes what Adam in his rebellion did for all mankind, both Jew and Gentile (Chapters 4-5).

Baptized into Christ, believers receive a new identity and live this out by faith (chapter 6). The power for the Christian life is not in obeying the Mosaic law but in trusting the Holy Spirit (chapters 7-8). We now live in this world confident that nothing can separate us from the love of God in Christ Jesus our Lord.

Does Paul's gospel mean that God has voided His promises to Israel? Certainly not! Throughout her history God has shown Himself to be sovereign. He is the God of the surprise; we cannot calculate or control Him. Even though Israel rejected her Messiah, God used this to bring the gospel to the Gentiles. When their full number has come in, then the Jews too will be saved. God will be shown to be faithful in His covenant to Israel and faithful to the Gentiles as well (chapters 9-11).

Based on this gospel we are to give our bodies to God in worship and to live together, Jew and Gentile, as members of the body of Christ. Gifted for ministry, a new quality of relationships will develop allowing believers to live boldly in the world, yet supportive to the state as it fulfills its God-ordained functions (chapters 12-13).

Living together in the body of Christ means that Christians are to defend each other's conscience in relative matters of custom, always acting from faith. The strong must help the weak and both are to glorify God together (chapter 14). Paul concludes with his plans to go to Jerusalem, Rome and Spain and sends greetings to a host of friends (chapters 15-16).

His letter then is an exposition of the gospel to both Jew and Gentile. Both are accepted by faith in Jesus Christ. Both are to live out their new life together, caring for each other. It is in this context that we examine the role of women in Paul's letter to the Romans.

Romans 1:26-27

[26] *For this reason God gave them up to dishonorable passions. Their women exchanged natural relations for unnatural,*

²⁷and the men likewise gave up natural relations with women and were consumed with passion for one another, men committing shameless acts with men and receiving in their own persons the due penalty for their error.

In the context, Paul speaks of the wrath of God against human sin (1:18). This wrath is deserved because mankind has substituted idols for the true knowledge of God (1:23). The destruction of our relationship with God reverberates in the destruction of our relationships with each other. Losing our center in God, we lose our identity. When we no longer know who God is, we no longer know who we are. This is judged by God's "passive" wrath. He lets sin run its course: "For this reason God gave them up...."

One sign of sin is homosexuality. The loss of identity is seen in the violation of our sexuality. No longer do women and men know how to relate properly to each other.

While Paul does not condemn homosexuality as the worst sin, he does show it to be the most obvious illustration of the loss of identity. Both lesbians and homosexuals are treated equally. Sin is universal and it distorts both sexes without favoritism. If anything, the stress is on the corruption of the male. Both male and female, however, express their alienation from God in the extreme form of losing their sexual identity. Both stand under the judgment of God for this, "God gave them up....," and both, to be sure, are the objects of God's grace and mercy in Jesus Christ.

Romans 4:19-21

¹⁹He [Abraham] did not weaken in faith when he considered his own body, which was as good as dead because he was about a hundred years old, or when he considered the barrenness of Sarah's womb. ²⁰No distrust made him waver concerning the promise of God, but he grew strong in his faith as he gave glory to God, ²¹fully convinced that God was able to do what He had promised.

Paul's intention is to show that his gospel is no last-minute innovation by God. Father Abraham, the founder of the Jewish people, lived by faith and was reckoned righteous because of it (4:3). He too received life from the dead, having his son in old age when both his and his wife's natural resources were exhausted. His own body and Sarah's womb were "as good as dead." But by faith they received the miracle of a son.

Abraham and Sarah are shown here by Paul to be equally impotent. While the stress is on Abraham, Sarah is also mentioned. Both are examples of those reduced to nothing so that God could make something of them (Martin Luther). Sarah stands with Abraham as a witness to the miracle of God.

Romans 7:1-3

¹Do you not know, brethren - for I am speaking to those who know the law - that the law is binding on a person only during his life? ²Thus a married woman is bound by law to her husband as long as he lives; but if her husband dies she is discharged from the law concerning the husband. ³Accordingly, she will be called an adulteress if she lives with another man while her husband is alive. But if her husband dies she is freed from that law, and if she marries another man she is not an adulteress.

Paul offers an illustration for the radical nature of the Christian life: we who are in Christ have died to the old life (including the law), thus it can make no claim upon us.

To illustrate his point the Apostle uses a Jewish woman who is bound to her husband until he dies. If she has an affair with another man while he lives, she is guilty of adultery. After he is deceased, however, she is free to marry again. Paul then goes on to apply this to the Christian who has died to the law in the death of Christ and who now lives a new life in Him.

What is noteworthy here is that Paul draws his illustration from marriage, focusing on the woman. She is bound to her husband through his lifetime as all outside of Christ are bound to the law. She is called into submission to him; the word "married" itself means literally "under man" (7:2). Here the traditional, patriarchal view is assumed.

In the illustration the woman, however, now becomes the paradigm of our new life in Christ and our new relationship with Him. As death frees her to marry another so the believer dies to the old order and arises into the new, crossing the great divide of sin and death into Christ Himself: "Likewise, my brethren, you have died to the law through the body of Christ, so that you may belong to another, to Him who has been raised from the dead in order that we may bear fruit for God" (7:4).

If Paul had a rabbinic bias against women (such as the first century Rabbi Hillel, "Many women, many superstitions")[1], he probably would have chosen a different illustration. A woman, however, becomes an analogy for the Christian experience of all believers.

Romans 9:6-13

[6]*But it is not as though the word of God had failed. For not all who are descended from Israel belong to Israel, [7]and not all are children of Abraham because they are his descendants; but "Through Isaac shall your descendants be named." [8]This means that it is not the children of the flesh who are the children of God, but the children of the promise are reckoned as descendants. [9]For this is what the promise said, "About this time I will return and Sarah shall have a son." [10]And not only so, but also when Rebecca had conceived children by*

one man, our forefather Isaac, [11]though they were not yet born and had done nothing either good or bad, in order that God's purpose of election might continue, not because of works but because of his call, [12]she was told, "the elder will serve the younger." [13]As it is written, "Jacob I loved, but Esau I hated."

Paul confronts the question of Israel's rejecting her Messiah in Romans 9-11. His answer, in part, is that throughout her history God has had His surprises. He does not fulfill our cultural or theological expectations. While the Jews were offended by a crucified Messiah, this was God's way of redeeming the world.

God's surprises, however, did not begin with the coming of Christ. Throughout her history, Israel was taught the unexpected grace of God. Abraham had Ishmael as a son of the flesh, but it was Isaac, the son of God's promise, who continued the line of God's people. God's word to Abraham was, "About this time I will return and Sarah shall have a son." It is through Sarah then that grace is given (see 4:19-21 above).

Again in Rebecca we see God's sovereign surprise as He elects to continue His work through the younger son Jacob, "She was told, 'the elder will serve the younger' " (9:12). This contradicts all of the legal and cultural expectations of the time.

While Paul mentions Abraham and Isaac, he also mentions Sarah and Rebecca. Both men and women are the objects of God's gracious work. Both men and women are vehicles of His unexpected revelation. Both men and women are the subjects of His sovereign will. But it is especially through the women that the promise becomes real - the fruit of their wombs bears God's purpose to the next generation and continues His saving history which culminates in Christ.

Romans 9:25

[25]*As indeed he says in Hosea, "Those who were not my people I will call 'my people', and her who was not beloved I will call 'my beloved'."*

God's mercy, Paul shows, is for both Jew and Gentile. This is foreshadowed in Hosea whose harlot wife bears children called "Not pitied" and "Not my people" (Hosea 1:2-9). These symbolic names represent God's rejection of Israel. Yet as Hosea loves a harlot, so God loves the unfaithful Israelites and the promise comes that they will be restored again. "Not my people," representing a faithless daughter, will be called "My beloved." God's mercy will triumph over His judgment.

The ultimate expression of grace is not only in calling back wayward Israel, but in calling the Gentiles to Christ. Thus in restoring the rejected, God prepares Israel for the inclusion of the Gentiles.

In using this prophecy Paul follows Hosea in designating both the male, "Not my people," and the female, "Not beloved" ("not pitied" - R.S.V., Hosea 1:6). The gospel is for Jew and Gentile, male and female. There is no distinction. This is symbolized in Hosea's children and used by the Apostle to represent both God's grace and the universality of the gospel.

Romans 16:1-2

[1]*I commend to you our sister Phoebe, a deaconess of the church at Cenchreae, *[2]*that you may receive her in the Lord as befits the saints, and help her in whatever she may require from you, for she has been a helper of many and of myself as well.*

Phoebe is commended by Paul to the church at Rome. This is an official recommendation and endorsement of her ministry (compare II Corinthians 3:1-2). She is a sister in the faith and holds an official function as "deaconess" or "minister." The word is masculine here and is the same one used by Paul to speak of himself and Apollos (I Corinthians 3:5), Tychicus (Ephesians 6:21; Colossians 4:7), and Timothy (I Timothy 4:6). He can even speak of Christ as becoming a "servant ('minister'-'deacon') to the circumcised" (Romans 15:8).

A "deacon" is a minister "of a new covenant ...in the Spirit" (II Corinthians 3:6). Paul was made a "deacon" of the gospel according to the gift of God's grace (Ephesians 3:7). Timothy as a "deacon of Christ Jesus" is to be "nourished on the words of the faith and of the good doctrine which you have followed" (I Timothy 4:6). Thus while "deacon" originally meant "table waiter" in Classical Greek, Paul views deacons as those who are responsible for the gospel, the ministers of the word of God. While their function includes ministering to physical needs these are never separated from spiritual needs (see Acts 6-7 where Stephen cares for the food distribution and preaches).

Phoebe, then, is to be received and honored in the Lord and given hospitality and practical help for her ministry. She is commended for the way in which she has served others, including Paul himself.

The following points emerge from this crucial passage. First, Phoebe is a minister in the church of Cenchreae. Her title, "deacon" is in the masculine; there are therefore no linguistic or theological grounds to distinguish between her and other male "ministers." Second, she is to be honored and aided by the Romans. Paul assumes that they will have no problem welcoming her as a "minister." In other words, Phoebe is no isolated phenomenon. Third, she has a ministry recognized for its fruit; "she has been a helper of many." This is a clear sign of God's call and blessing upon her. Fourth, her ministry has such value that it extends beyond her own congregation. She will be expected to minister in Rome. Fifth, she has ministered to Paul, that is, he has been the object of her physical and spiritual aid. Phoebe is likely carrying this letter to Rome for him.

There is no reason to suppose that Phoebe does not hold a ministerial office. She undoubtedly performs ministerial functions which are equally shared by Paul and others. Thus no sexual qualifications are made here for such ministry.

Romans 16:3-5

³*Greet Prisca and Aquila, my fellow workers in Christ Jesus,* ⁴*who risked their necks for my life, to whom not only I but also all the churches of the Gentiles give thanks;* ⁵*greet also the church in their house.*

Paul begins his farewell greetings by singling out a couple who have played a major role in his ministry (see I Corinthians 16:19; Act 18:2, 18:18, etc.). In so doing he names the woman, Prisca, first. He also titles both she and her husband as "fellow workers" ("co-workers"), a term of equality elsewhere used of Paul and Apollos (I Corinthians 3:9), and Euodia, Syntyche, "True Yokefellow" and Clement (Philippians 4:2-3).

Risking their lives for Paul, Prisca and Aquila are recognized among all the Gentile churches, and share in the ministry of a church in their home. Paul gives them both the highest commendation.

Nowhere is it suggested that Prisca is inferior to or under the authority of Aquila in ministry. To the contrary, she shares a title and task of equality as a "fellow-worker." She is a fellow-worker in suffering and in church building and is universally recognized as such.

Romans 16:6

⁶*Greet Mary, who has worked hard among you.*

Paul designates Mary as working hard among the Romans. The verb is used elsewhere by the Apostle to describe ministerial labor in the gospel. In 16:12 it is applied to another woman, Persis, "who has worked hard in the Lord." In I Corinthians 15:10 it capsualizes apostolic labors. In I Thessalonians 5:12 the church is called to respect those who "labor among you and are over you in the Lord...."

The prepositional phrase translated "among you" is rendered "over you" in Galatians 4:11 in the R.S.V. It is possible that Mary had some overseeing responsibility in her ministry.

Romans 16:7

⁷Greet Andronicus and Junias, my kinsmen and my fellow prisoners; they are men of note among the apostles, and they were in Christ before me.

The unresolved issue is whether Junias in Greek is a masculine contraction of Junianus or the feminine Junia. The spelling in the original language is the same for either possibility. Furthermore, the phrase "they are men of note" literally reads "they are of note." "Men" is absent in the Greek, and is inserted by the translators. Thus Paul could be referring to a woman here, quite probably a husband-wife team.

This would mean that Junia is a "kinsman," that is, a Jew. She is also a "fellow prisoner," that is, she like Paul had suffered incarceration for her faith in Christ. Most surprising, Junia is also an apostle, an early convert even before Paul. This has led most commentators to render the proper name as the masculine Junias rather than Junia. While a final decision cannot be reached from the text, why must we suppose that no woman could be called an apostle by Paul? In the wider sense of the word, an apostle is one who is sent with a commission. II Corinthians 8:23 speaks of those who are bringing a gift of money to the Jerusalem church as "messengers (Greek-'apostles') of the churches."

Since, however, no special task is mentioned for Andronicus and Junias (or Junia), their apostleship would be from Christ, sealed in being eyewitnesses to the resurrection of the Lord (see Acts 1:21-26; I Corinthians 9:1 and 15:3-8). This is also substantiated by the time of their conversion (before Paul's) which would make them among the first believers after the resurrection of Christ.

In Romans 16 Paul has already mentioned one married couple and two single women, thus the naming of another woman would not be unexpected in the context. Furthermore, it would be improbable that two of the earliest male converts would still be together about 25 years later so as to be mentioned in one greeting. The double greeting is much more likely if they are a married couple who have been sharing their witness to Christ through all the intervening years. Only an extra-Biblical assumption that a woman could not be an apostle keeps most commentators from reading Junias as Junia. The church father Chrysostom had no such bias. He writes, "And indeed to be Apostles at all is a great thing. But to be even amongst these of note, just consider what a great encomium this is! But they were of note owing to their works, to their achievements. Oh! how great is the devotion of this woman, that she should be even counted worthy of the appellation of apostle!"[2]

Romans 16:12

[12]*Greet those workers in the Lord, Tryphaena and Tryphosa. Greet the beloved Persis, who has worked hard in the Lord.*

Tryphaena and Tryphosa are probably sisters. They along with Persis are designated as workers in the Lord. As with Mary in 16:6, these women all engaged in ministerial activity. This is established by calling them "workers." The use of the verb suggests function more than office. They are commended for their work and the results of their labors. Persis is also singled out as "beloved." Paul is unafraid of warm, personal references in his relationships to women as well as to men.

Romans 16:13

[13] *Greet Rufus, eminent in the Lord, also his mother and mine.*

The mother of Rufus is mentioned here as mothering Paul in times past. Since Paul is an old man and we hear nowhere else of his having a brother Rufus, this mother is probably not physically related to the Apostle. Her service to him has been one of love and care and this is another glimpse into Paul's warm relationships with women.

Romans 16:15

[15] *Greet Philologus, Julia, Nereus and his sister, and Olympas, and all the saints who are with them.*

Julia is a common Roman female name. She is greeted along with the sister of Nereus. This concludes the 8 or possibly 9 women (if we add Junia) singled out for greetings by Paul in Romans 16.

In Conclusion

In this letter, Paul expounds upon the unity of Jew and Gentile in Christ. They are one in their descent from Adam, they are one in their sin, they are one in justification by faith, and they are to live together as one in the body of Christ.

Although the Jews have a special priority in God's call and covenant, they, like the Gentiles, can only know God through the gospel of His Son.

To illustrate the great themes of the gospel in this letter, Paul employs Old Testament figures and prophecies, the example of marriage, and cultural observations which all relate to women.

Thus, Romans retains its balance in commending the gospel to all races and to both sexes. It is fitting that in his final greetings the Apostle endorses and salutes both men and women who share in the ministry of this gospel in the church and in the world.

I CORINTHIANS

Introduction

I Corinthians is written to a church in danger of bitter division. Problems rage like flames in a forest of dry timber. Paul's authority is under question, his style of preaching and ministry are suspect and his responsibility in money matters is doubted. The order of the church is breaking down. Some in Corinth boast of the "Christian freedom" displayed by a man living in incest. Others are taking fellow Christians to court. Some continue to visit prostitutes. Others prove their freedom by eating meat offered to idols. Women are worshipping immodestly. Drunkenness is staining the celebration of the Lord's Supper. Spiritual gifts are abused provoking jealousy. Tongues is valued for its ecstasy rather than prophecy for its edification. In sum, both personal morality and congregational life are collapsing.

The division and chaos in the church come from a misunderstanding of the gospel. The Corinthians are in danger of moving beyond the "word of the cross," Christ crucified, and into a spiritual theology of mystical exaltation. They desire to leave behind the physical, historical core of the faith accomplished in the work of Christ, and thus they deny a future bodily resurrection for believers. The Corinthians want resurrection now as an ecstatic event which will deliver them from history and place them in "spiritual orbit" beyond this world. Tongues is valued for this purpose, not for edifying the believer or the church. Once in ecstasy, issues of the unity of the believers, personal morality, order in worship, and the factual nature of the gospel become irrelevant.

Paul rebukes the church for this false enthusiasm. He calls the Corinthians back to the cross and the resurrection of Christ (Chapters 1 and 15). He calls the Corinthians to a personal morality which will display the character of God in the world (chapters 5-10). He calls the Corinthians to order in the church that will build them up rather than trip them out (chapters 11-12 and 14). Finally, he calls the Corinthians to a love which will restore the harmony and unity of their Christian body and make the gospel believable once again (chapter 13). It is in this context that we will examine Paul and his teaching on women in the church.

I Corinthians 1:10-11

[10]*I appeal to you, brethren, by the name of our Lord Jesus Christ, that all of you agree and that there be no dissensions among you, but that you be united in the same mind and the same judgment.* [11]*For it has been reported to me by Chloe's people that there is quarreling among you, my brethren.*

Paul, now in Ephesus (16:8), has received a report on the Corinthians from Chloe's people. Chloe is a woman member of either the church of Corinth or the church of Ephesus. At first reading it is more probable that her people belong to Corinth for this would give them immediate knowledge of the problems of division there. However, since a delegation of men including Stephanas, Fortunatus, and Achaicus has come from Corinth (16:17-18), undoubtedly bringing the Corinthians' letter which Paul answers starting in 7:1, it is strange that these men are not the source for the report of division. Perhaps Paul singled out Chloe's people because, not being Corinthians, it would not appear that they were talking down their own church.

Chloe's people may be immediate members of her family, members of the church in her house, or servants belonging to her. Undoubtedly they were Christians and thus probably members of

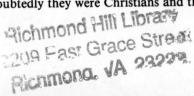

the same church fellowship to which she belonged. It is interesting that a woman is designated as having authority over the delegation reporting on the chaos in Corinth.

I Corinthians 5:1

¹*It is actually reported that there is immorality among you, and of a kind that is not found even among pagans; for a man is living with his father's wife.*

A shocking abuse of Christian freedom is dealt with here as a male member of the church lives in incest with his stepmother. Some even boast about it (5:2). The man's "father's wife" is not mentioned again. It is he, not she, who is to be judged for this travesty and expelled from the congregation (5:3-5). The absence of judgment upon her probably means that she is not a Christian, and therefore the church has no responsibility for her. It also clearly means that the man is given responsibility for this offensive behavior which receives the severest rebuke. Notice too that Paul's goal is that the discipline given be ultimately redemptive. The man is to be turned over to Satan (by excommunication) that his soul may be saved (5:5).

I Corinthians 6:15-16

¹⁵*Do you not know that your bodies are members of Christ? Shall I therefore take the members of Christ and make them members of a prostitute? Never!* ¹⁶*Do you not know that he who joins himself to a prostitute becomes one body with her? For, as it is written, "The two shall become one."*

Some Corinthian men continue to visit prostitutes. Their abuse of Christian freedom is based upon the materialistic position that the body will be destroyed (6:13); thus they can do with it as they please. "No," Paul retorts. The body is destined not for destruction but for the Lord: its goal is resurrection (6:14). Furthermore, when we are united to Christ our total selves, including our bodies, are united to Him and become members of Him (6:15). Paul denies any *ultimate dualism* that saves the soul but denies the value of the body.

Since our bodies are united to Christ (compare Romans 12:1-2), can they at the same time be united to a prostitute? Paul responds, "Never." This is not arguable; it is unthinkable. God's intention for our sexual union according to Genesis 2:24 is that we become a single entity, "one flesh": "For as it is written, 'The two shall become one' " (6:16). How then can Christ be joined to a prostitute? The sanctity of Christ, the sanctity of our bodies as members of Christ, and the sanctity of sexual union mitigate against this. Since man and woman become one in intercourse, prostitution is a violation of that oneness. Both God's intention in creating us as sexual beings and our dignity in belonging to Christ are marred by infidelity. Paul is neither anti-sex nor anti-female here. He opposes the violation of human sexuality and of womanhood by those who market sex as a commodity to be consumed. We have a higher destiny than such exploitation. We are members of Christ and must therefore behave in that way. Prostitution is the abuse of sex, the self, and Christ. It is prostitution that the Apostle attacks. The Christian is to have nothing of this because God gives him a higher view of his body and of sexual union.

I Corinthians 7:1-5

¹Now concerning the matters about which you wrote. It is well for a man not to touch a woman. ²But because of the temptation to immorality, each man should have his own wife and each woman her own husband. ³The husband should give to his wife her conjugal rights, and likewise the wife to her husband. ⁴For the wife does not rule over her own body, but the husband does; likewise the husband does not rule over his own body, but the wife does. ⁵Do not refuse one another except perhaps by agreement for a season, that you may devote yourselves to prayer; but then come together again, lest Satan tempt you through lack of self-control.

Now Paul turns to a letter written to him from Corinth, answering specific questions point by point. His first response concerns celibacy, sexual relations in marriage, mixed marriages, the betrothed and widows.

The Apostle begins with an affirmation of celibacy: "It is well for a man not to touch a woman." The euphemism "to touch," means "to have sexual intercourse with." Paul obviously does not prohibit any physical contact between the sexes (compare I Corinthians 16:20; II Corinthians 13:12; I Thessalonians 5:26). The word "well" is a subjective word meaning "advantageous"; it does not mean "good" in a moral or objective sense (see I Corinthians 7:36; "let them marry - it is no sin."). It is well not to marry because of the crisis time in which Christians live between Christ's first and second comings where the time is short and the form of the world is passing away (7:25-31). It is also well because the celibate is free for total devotion to the Lord (7:32-35). However it is "well" only for those who have received the gift *(charisma)* of celibacy like Paul (7:7). Apart from this, marriage is the norm. Thus the Apostle immediately writes, "But because of the temptation to immorality, each man should have his own wife, and each woman her own husband."

Paul tells us not why marriage has been instituted but for whom marriage has been instituted (John Calvin). Marriage is the functional solution for those tempted to immorality and the Apostle assumes that they will be the large majority of people: "each man...each woman...."

It is important to note that throughout this text Paul expresses the equality of the sexes. While each man should have his own wife the Apostle immediately balances this with each woman having her own husband. Paul cares for the fidelity of both. Paul knows the needs of both. Paul offers the solution for both. There is no sexism here. A single woman who is tempted needs a husband every bit as much as a single man needs a wife. 7:2 reveals complete symmetry of grammar and content as the Apostle deals with both sexes.

This symmetry continues in 7:3-4 where Paul goes on to speak of sexual responsibility in marriage. The husband is to give to the wife her complete sexual rights and she is to give the same to her husband. In their union the husband now rules over his wife's body and likewise "the husband does not rule over his own body, but the wife does."

This surprising expression of sexual equality and surrender again presupposes and defends the absolute equality of the sexes at their most intimate encounter. Each is to surrender his or her body to the other partner. Each is lord over the other's body. Paul presupposes that mutual love and self-giving will be expressed in our sexuality. No ego-trip, no will to power, no seduction or rape is tolerated. Here is mutual surrender. Here is the meeting of each other's sexual needs and desires. Here is tremendous freedom and joy in sexual union. Here is the physical expression of the one flesh (see 6:16). Here is the gospel in action—self-less love, giving to receive. The last thing in Paul's mind is male-dominance or egotism. If sexual love expresses our identity, then Christian sexual relations express the identity of mutual surrender and the employment of each other's bodies for sexual fulfillment. As Christ gave Himself for us, so we give ourselves for each other.

The only limitation on physical love in marriage is a mutually agreed upon brief period of separation for spiritual discipline (7:5). Notice that it must be a mutual agreement, not the decision of the male alone. Each must care for the needs and fidelity of the other. The time period must be brief so that Satan can have no opportunity through the frustrated sexual needs of one partner.

Since Paul holds to such equality and mutuality in marriage and sexual expression, we must assume that this primal equality will manifest itself throughout the marriage relationship. Marriage here is indeed a partnership.

I Corinthians 7:8-9

[8] To the unmarried and the widows I say that it is well for them to remain single as I do. [9] But if they cannot exercise self-control, they should marry. For it is better to marry than to be aflame with passion.

Paul now turns to the Corinthians' questions about the unmarried and the widows. He advocates celibacy for them following his own example. This is to be lived out, however, only if they have been gifted for it as Paul has been (7:6-7). Apart from this they are to marry. This is part of God's answer to lust. Again there is no sexual discrimination here. The unmarried may be male or female. The widows need not marry for economic, social, or religious status. If gifted, they too may remain single, modeling their lives after the Apostle (see also 7:36-40).

I Corinthians 7:10-11

[10] To the married I give charge, not I but the Lord, that the wife should not separate from her husband [11] (but if she does, let her remain single or else be reconciled to her husband) - and that the husband should not divorce his wife.

Concerning the married Paul has a word from the Lord, meaning the tradition which goes back to the historical Jesus (see Matthew 5:32, 19:3-9; Mark 10:2-12; Luke 16:18).

The heart of this teaching is that marriage should not be broken. The wife should not leave her husband and the husband should not divorce his wife. Notice again the symmetry of thought and expression (compare 7:2-4). If the wife does separate herself she should remain single, thus avoiding adultery, or be reconciled to her husband.

While in these verses Paul speaks of the wife's "separation" and the husband's "divorce," in verses 13 and 15 he interchanges the verbs: "she should not divorce him"; "But if the unbelieving partner desires to separate, let it be so...." Thus, contrary to Jewish law, the Apostle sees either sex initiating divorce, a process which was possible in the Roman world. Therefore Paul imposes no Jewish tradition upon the church. But he does impose God's intention that marriage be lasting in the unity of the one flesh (Genesis 2:24) and he exhorts both partners to faithfulness.

I Corinthians 7:12-16

[12]*To the rest I say, not the Lord, that if any brother has a wife who is an unbeliever, and she consents to live with him, he should not divorce her.* [13]*If any woman has a husband who is an unbeliever, and he consents to live with her, she should not divorce him.* [14]*For the unbelieving husband is consecrated through his wife, and the unbelieving wife is consecrated through her husband. Otherwise, your children would be unclean, but as it is they are holy.* [15]*But if the unbelieving partner desires to separate, let it be so; in such a case the brother or sister is not bound. For God has called us to peace.* [16]*Wife, how do you know whether you will save your husband? Husband, how do you know whether you will save your wife?*

What then of mixed marriages - where one partner is a believer and the other an unbeliever? For this Paul has no historical teaching from Jesus, but he exercises his apostolic authority.

Generally, mixed marriages are to be continued by the believing partner unless the unbeliever desires dissolution. The reasons for this are that the believer is a means of grace to the unbelieving partner: the believer consecrates ("sets apart") the unbeliever. Paul thinks of this almost physically. As a Christian joined to a prostitute actually joins Christ to her (see 6:15-16 above), so a Christian joined to a non-Christian in marriage brings Christ in relation to the partner. This means that the children from such a union are holy; that is, they belong to the Lord, but this does not mean that the believer saves the unbeliever (or that parents save their children) apart from his or her will. This is clear as Paul concludes with the rhetorical questions: "Wife, how do you know whether you will save your husband? Husband, how do you know whether you will save your wife?"

Believers in the marriage union bring unbelievers within range of God's people and God's grace. Both unbelieving partners and children stand in a special relationship to the gospel. This is both theologically and sociologically true. Such families are continually exposed to Christ through the Christians who pray, love and witness to them.

Throughout this passage Paul deals with each sex symmetrically and equally. As in 7:2-4 women have equal standing and equal responsibility with men in marriage.

I Corinthians 7:25-31

25Now concerning the unmarried, I have no command of the Lord, but I give my opinion as one who by the Lord's mercy is trustworthy. 26I think that in view of the impending distress it is well for a person to remain as he is. 27Are you bound to a wife? Do not seek to be free. Are you free from a wife? Do not seek marriage. 28But if you marry, you do not sin, and if a girl marries she does not sin. Yet those who marry will have worldly troubles, and I would spare you that. 29I mean, brethren, the appointed time has grown very short; from now on, let those who have wives live as though they had none,

---

30and those who mourn as though they were not mourning, and those who rejoice as though they were not rejoicing, and those who buy as though they had no goods, 31and those who deal with the world as though they had no dealings with it. For the form of this world is passing away.

Paul argues, not from the tradition of Jesus, but from his own gift and authority, for celibacy (7:7; 25). Since the Christian lives in the crisis time between the first and second comings of Christ, where the time is short, and the form of the world is passing away (7:26, 29, 31), his best position is the freedom of a single state.

If, however, he is married he should not seek to be free. If single, he should not seek marriage (7:27). Marriage, while not sinful (7:28) is inexpedient. The Christian is to live in this crisis time disengaged from the traps of this temporal world. His identity and joy must not come from the "passing show" of this age. Thus not marriage, nor mourning, nor rejoicing, nor dealings with the world are to claim any ultimate loyalty - for all is passing away.

The male is addressed in 7:27; he is neither to break his marriage nor to seek a new marriage. Both sexes are addressed in 7:28: "But if you marry, you do not sin, and if a girl marries she does not sin." Again Paul reveals the equality of the sexes. Neither is guilty of sin if he or she chooses to marry. His statement is consistently symmetrical (compare 7:2-4, 10-11, 13-16).

The eschatological motivation for this paragraph bears note. Some denounce the Apostle because he appears to base his argument against marriage upon the speedy return of Christ. Since he was proven wrong by time, it is then held that his theology fails. Paul speaks of this in three verses:

1. 7:26 "I think that in view of the impending (or present) distress it is well for a person to remain as he is."

2. 7:29 "I mean, brethren, the appointed time has grown very short...."
3. 7:31 "For the form of this world is passing away."

What then does Paul mean by each of these statements?

The first, the impending or present ("imminent") distress is an apocalyptic term indicating Christian existence in this world. God and Satan battle prior to the return of Christ and the end of this age. No necessary chronological time sequence, however, is presupposed. The church lives "between the times," in a conflict situation of "distress." This is always the setting for her life in this world (compare I Thessalonians 3:3-7).

The second, the shortness of the appointed time, tells us that the church lives in a time that bears the quality of the end within it because of the death and resurrection of Christ. In other words, the time (*kairos* - "season") *is* short (present tense verb), not because Paul has a date set for Christ's return, but because in Christ the final events of the end times have begun. Christ's death resolves the question of our position on the Day of Judgment (Romans 8:1). His resurrection begins the general resurrection of the dead, He is the "first fruits" of those who have slept (I Corinthians 15:20). Thus we live in a time of "distress" (7:26) and a time which reveals the end or goal of God's purpose (7:29). It has grown very short (literally it is "of the nature of being wrapped up"), because Jesus has come inaugurating the goal of God's salvation towards which all history heretofore has moved.

The third, the passing form of the world, needs little comment. The church lives in the consciousness that this age, this order, is passing away. No temporal moment, no worldly institution, has absolute value. In the coming of Christ, God reveals the world's bankruptcy as well as His divine purpose to unite us to the eternal order of His Son. The form of the world is passing away not because Christ will come soon, but because He has already come to reveal its transitory character and begin the consummation of all things.

Thus all Christians in all ages live in a period of distress, a period of the end times, and a period where it has been shown that the old world is passing away, even as the new world has dawned in Christ.

I Corinthians 7:32-35

[32]*I want you to be free from anxieties. The unmarried man is anxious about the affairs of the Lord, how to please the Lord;* [33]*but the married man is anxious about worldly affairs, how to please his wife,* [34]*and his interests are divided. And the unmarried woman or girl is anxious about the affairs of the Lord, how to be holy in body and spirit; but the married woman is anxious about worldly affairs, how to please her husband.* [35]*I say this for your own benefit, not to lay any restraint upon you, but to promote good order and to secure your undivided devotion to the Lord.*

Paul's further argument against marriage is determined by his purpose: "to promote good order and to secure your undivided devotion to the Lord" (7:35). The unmarried have the advantage of a single preoccupation - how to please the Lord. Their attention is not distracted by worldly matters.

The married man and woman, however, have to contend with their affairs in this world. Pleasing each other may replace or challenge pleasing the Lord. Divided interests will be the result.

In Paul's perceptive warning here, he again deals with both men and women equally. His desire is that both have undivided devotion to Christ. Neither is inferior to the other. Both are crucial in God's purpose. Marriage may be a hinderance to both. Celibacy may be the answer for both. The goal for all, celibate or married, must be "undivided devotion to the Lord" (7:35). This is the positive teaching of this passage. In sum, both the eschatological argument (7:25-31) and the practical argument (7:32-35) are used to expound the value of Paul's gift of celibacy for the church (7:7). Elsewhere, the Apostle will balance this with further teaching on marriage (see Ephesians 5:21-33).

I Corinthians 7:36-38

[36]*If any one thinks that he is not behaving properly toward his betrothed, if his passions are strong, and it has to be, let him do as he wishes; let them marry - it is no sin.* [37]*But whoever is firmly established in his heart, being under no necessity but having his desire under control, and has determined this in his heart, to keep her as his betrothed, he will do well.* [38]*So that he who marries his betrothed does well, and he who refrains from marriage will do better.*

Paul now gives directions to engaged couples. The word "betrothed" literally means "virgin." Some take this passage as referring to fathers with their virgin daughters since the verb in 7:38 may be rendered "give in marriage" rather than "marry."[1] Others hold that Paul is endorsing a spiritual betrothal, a kind of platonic Christian love which is to be surrendered if passion becomes too great.

Probably, however, Paul speaks of real engagements which are to be consummated when passion is strong. The focus here is on the male, the one section in I Corinthians 7 where the male/female symmetry is broken. Perhaps the Apostle addresses only the male because he assumes his initiative in consummating the marriage vow. The conclusion that "He who marries his betrothed...will do well, and he who refrains from marriage will do better," contains no moral, but a practical or functional judgment.

I Corinthians 7:39-40

[39]*A wife is bound to her husband as long as he lives. If the husband dies, she is free to be married to whom she wishes,*

only in the Lord. *⁴⁰But in my judgment she is happier if she remains as she is. And I think that I have the Spirit of God.*

Paul concludes this chapter addressing himself to widows. Again he argues against divorce (see 7:10-16). Death, however, terminates the marriage bond. The widow is then free to remarry "in the Lord," that is, to another Christian. Nevertheless, the Apostle encourages remaining in a single state for reasons previously given (see 7:25-35).

Notice that the widow is free to select her new mate as long as he is a believer. Again no male domination is expressed. A widow will be happier single, Paul supposes, adding with a note of sarcasm or understatement, rather than doubt: "And I think that I have the Spirit of God" (compare 2:6-16).

I Corinthians 9:3-5

³This is my defense to those who would examine me. ⁴Do we not have the right to our food and drink? ⁵Do we not have the right to be accompanied by a wife, as the other apostles and the brothers of the Lord and Cephas?

Employing the imagery of a law court, Paul, as the defense attorney, makes his case against the accusation that he has abused his apostolic rights by living a life of comfort and profiteering from the gospel. To the contrary, he responds, although having every right to make a living by the gospel, the Apostle, to avoid offense, refuses (9:15-18). He preaches "free of charge" (9:18).

In the course of his defense which centers on money matters, Paul mentions the right to travel with a wife. He reveals that he does not do so (thus undoubtedly unmarried, compare chapter 7), and also shows that the other apostles, Jesus' brothers and Cephas (Peter) were married. Thus marriage is the standard among the leadership of the church. The apostles apparently thought so highly of their wives that they normally traveled with them. No hint is expressed of the celibacy of the priesthood or of a disdain for marriage. On the contrary, Paul sacrifices this joy for the sake of his mission.

I Corinthian 11:2-16

²I commend you because you remember me in everything and maintain the traditions even as I have delivered them to you. ³But I want you to understand that the head of every man is Christ, the head of a woman is her husband, and the head of Christ is God. ⁴Any man who prays or prophesies with his head covered dishonors his head, ⁵but any woman who prays or prophesies with her head unveiled dishonors her head - it is the same as if her head were shaven. ⁶For if a woman will not veil herself, then she should cut off her hair: but if it is disgraceful for a woman to be shorn or shaven, let her wear a veil. ⁷For a man ought not to cover his head, since he is the image and glory of God; but woman is the glory of man. ⁸(For man was not made from woman, but woman from man. ⁹Neither was man created for woman, but woman for man.) ¹⁰That is why a woman ought to have a veil on her head, because of the angels. ¹¹(Nevertheless, in the Lord woman is not independent of man nor man of woman; ¹²for as woman was made from man, so man is now born of woman. And all things are from God.) ¹³Judge for yourselves; is it proper for a woman to pray to God with her head uncovered? ¹⁴Does not nature itself teach you that for a man to wear long hair is degrading to him, ¹⁵but if a woman has long hair, it is her pride? For her hair is given to her for a covering. ¹⁶If any one is disposed to be contentious, we recognize no other practice, nor do the churches of God.

At this point in the letter Paul deals with specific abuses in worship among the Corinthians. He begins with women unveiling themselves while praying and prophesying (11:3-16), and then turns to drunkenness and disorder at the Lord's Supper (11:17-

34). This is followed by confronting the Corinthians' abuse of spiritual gifts including the undue stress on some to the depreciation of others (12:1-31) and their loveless use of them (13:1-13). Then Paul deals with the problem of exercising tongues without interpretation (14:1-25), and concludes with the church's disorder in worship (14:26-40).

The Apostle begins 11:3-16 from the general and probably cross-cultural (Jew and Gentile) position that women in public are to be veiled.[2] On this Sir William Ramsay writes, "In Oriental lands the veil is the power and the honour and dignity of the woman. With the veil on her head she can go anywhere in security and profound respect. She is not seen; it is a mark of thoroughly bad manners to observe a veiled woman in the street. She is alone. The rest of the people around her are non-existent to her....But without the veil the woman is a thing of nought, whom anyone may insult....A woman's authority and dignity vanish along with the all-covering veil that she discards."[3] Thus for Paul, Christian freedom cannot mean unveiled women who violate the general order of society. The church is not an enthusiastic cult abrogating the common life. Paul's dictum, "Give no offense to Jews or to Greeks or to the church of God, just as I try to please all men in everything I do, not seeking my own advantage, but that of the many, that they may be saved" (10:32-33), is here applied to women in worship.

The discussion begins by establishing that there is a divine order of hierarchy of headship. God is the head of Christ (literally, "the Messiah"), Christ is the head of man and the husband is the head of his wife.

Headship does not so much mean superiority or rule as it means source or origin.[4] For example, in Ephesians 5:23ff Christ is the head of the church because as its Savior He brings it into existence. In Ephesians 4:15-16 Christ as the head nourishes His body as it grows up into Him. Since the head is the source of life, when Paul writes that "the head of every man is Christ," he means that man lives in dependence upon Christ strengthened and sustained by him. So Christ also lives in dependence upon God and so also the wife lives in dependence upon her husband. Christ establishes His headship by giving Himself, not by taking or possessing. He exercises His headship by saving us; this is His glory and this is the model for the headship of husbands to their wives.

The husband shows his dependence upon Christ (and thus his dignity) by worshipping unveiled (11:4), "since he is the image and glory of God" (11:7). The expression of this dependence, which is his glory, lies in being bare-headed.

The wife's dependence upon her husband is reflected in her worshipping veiled (11:5). As it is shameful for her to be shaven or have short hair - signs of disgrace and excommunication from the community[5] - so it is shameful for her to worship unveiled, since "woman is the glory of man" (11:7) and symbolizes her dependence upon him through her veil (11:10). Thus she would be stepping out of the established order if she cast her veil aside, like a prostitute or widow. This would be an abuse of her freedom in Christ.

Paul grounds his argument for the veiling of women in (1) the doctrine of creation (11:7-9) and (2) nature or custom (11:13-16). Let us look at each of these points.

While it is true that creation reveals the unity and equality of the sexes (Genesis 1:27), it also reveals their diversity (Genesis 2:18-25). It is this that Paul focuses upon here in drawing the conclusion of woman's dependency upon man. Man is "the image and glory of God but woman is the glory of man" (11:7). Paul justifies woman's dependent position from two points: she is secondary chronologically, being made after man, and she is secondary functionally, being made for man (11:8-9).[6]

Not only is this true in creation, it is also true by observation. "Judge for yourselves" (11:13), that is, "Look around you."

The way women wear their hair and their pride in it also symbolizes in nature or custom that they are dependent upon man (11:14-15). Thus long hair is the equivalent of the veil. What then can be said of Paul's teaching up to this point?

In basing the differentiation of the sexes upon Genesis 2:18-25 the Apostle has applied part but not all of the doctrine of creation. In Genesis 1:27 both sexes are made in the image of God. Nevertheless, Genesis 1 does not void Genesis 2; they are complementary, both teaching important truths. That God gave each sex independent and equal value, creating both in His image is one essential truth (Genesis 1:27).[7] That God created the sexes for each other and provided for the needs of both in their union in "one flesh", however, is another essential truth (Genesis 2:18-25). Neither should be valued at the expense of the other.

Since Paul is arguing for the dependence of woman at this point and not making a full theological statement about male and female, he writes only that "woman is the glory of man" (11:7). This is seen in her function as being created "for man" and reflecting the image of God in him. If this text stood alone woman would seem depreciated. Yet part (and only part) of the Biblical revelation in Genesis 2 is that God intended the family unit from creation and man is incomplete without a companion fit for him who will fulfill the totality of his needs in the union of the one flesh.

Since both man and woman are created in the image of God in Genesis 1 and both become one flesh in Genesis 2 (thus sharing the image singly and together), there is no ultimate conflict between the opening chapters of Genesis. Yet the stress in Genesis 2 is on the woman created to fulfill the incomplete man who is neither independent sexually nor socially. Marriage, sexual union, and the re-creation of the family unit are God's general intentions for the race. Sex in marriage issuing in children is the sign of God's blessing upon the race. The created needs for companionship are optimally met in marriage, the total union of "one flesh." Thus the differentiation of the sexes is as important as their equality.

Paul's argument up to this point supports the general cultural attitudes, represents the position on women from Genesis 2, follows traditional Jewish interpretation, and upholds the differentiation of the sexes. Woman as dependent upon man is not grounded in the economic order of man as the provider and woman as the child-bearer. It is grounded in God's intention in creation, in the hierarchical structure of reality. Does this then mean that the conflict between the sexes and the secondary position of woman due to creation (as simply the glory of man) is the eternal order of God? Although Paul seems to hold this, he also takes decisive steps beyond this position. This his modern opponents fail to see.

At the beginning of the passage the Apostle teaches that wives relate to husbands as Christ relates to God. This can in no way be seen as a depreciated position. This gives wives inestimable value. Paul also advances beyond the traditional position on women in two other important respects.

First, rather than women being untaught, segregated and silent in the church as they were in the synagogue, women are to be participants in worship through prayer and prophecy (11:5). Thus they are to express their spiritual gifts which are not bestowed according to sex, for the upbuilding of the congregation (see I Corinthians 12-14). At issue is not whether or not they are to speak, but their attire as they speak.

Second, the statement that woman is made from man and for man (11:8-9) is immediately qualified by the following, "Nevertheless, in the Lord woman is not independent of man nor man of woman; for as woman was made from man, so man is now born of woman. And all things are from God" (11:11-12). Not only then is woman dependent upon man, but man is also dependent upon woman. It is "in the Lord," in Christ, that the dependent position of women and the conflict between the sexes is resolved. Here Paul takes another decisive step beyond the Old Testament by grounding that step not in the creation account of Genesis 1 but in the redemptive work of Christ.

What then can be said in conclusion about this difficult yet crucial passage?

1. Paul upholds the cultural custom of women being veiled against a radical assertion of women's freedom which would offend both Jew and Gentile and make Christian women scandalous to the culture.

2. Paul implies from Genesis 2 that wives are to express their dependence upon their husbands and difference from them by veils and length of hair. "In the flesh," in the created order, the differentiation between the sexes is upheld. Thus Paul formally satisfies especially the Jewish Christians who have come from the synagogue to the church.

3. Paul shows that in Christ the created differences and the potential warfare between the sexes has now been transcended. Husbands express their headship even as Christ expresses His - by loving service. At the same time, women are inspired by the Spirit and gifted for worship and ministry in the body of Christ. Since they must exercise their spiritual gifts to edify the body, the Holy Spirit has broken through the old orders of creation and nature at this point. Thus women express their freedom in using their gifts. Their only responsibility now is to maintain the external order so as to give no offense. While the form is traditional, the content is radical. Women along with men bear the word of God to the congregation.

4. The external order, however, is not the final, unalterable order. The doctrine of creation from Genesis 2 cannot determine the order of the church or the position of women independent of the gospel of Christ. "Nature" or "custom" and "judging for yourself" may well change by age. It is redemption, "in the

Lord,'' that must determine the ultimate order of the church. Paul takes conservative males and Jews and moves them beyond the limitations of creation and the fall by showing them the equality of the sexes as found "in the Lord" (11:11-12). This equality is even mirrored in the act of childbirth. As man is now dependent upon woman for physical birth, so Paul finds in the order of creation itself a sign for the new equality accomplished in redemption, "in the Lord."

To summarize: in the realization of redemption the old orders of creation and nature have been broken through. Women now have spiritual gifts to be exercised in the church and in the Lord. Their equality with men is understood. Neither sex is to be independent of the other nor to be assimilated by the other. Neither sex can now claim priority: "As woman was made from man, so man is now born of woman. And all things are from God."[8]

I Corinthians 14:33^b-36

As in all the churches of the saints, ³⁴the women should keep silence in the churches. For they are not permitted to speak, but should be subordinate, as even the law says. ³⁵If there is anything they desire to know, let them ask their husbands at home. For it is shameful for a woman to speak in church. ³⁶What! Did the word of God originate with you, or are you the only ones it has reached?

In I Corinthians 14 Paul continues to order the worship of the church. The gift of prophecy is to be preferred over tongues because it edifies the whole congregation (14:4). Tongues is to be employed in private unless the gift of interpretation is also given during corporate worship (14:28). In its absence the tongues speaker is to be silent, praying only to himself and God. As a further directive against chaos in worship Paul commands the silence of women. What does he mean by this?

At first reading, it appears that the Apostle simply teaches that women are not to speak in church, that is, they are to have no role in leadership in the congregation. They are to be subordinate to the men (14:34); it is shameful for them to speak out (14:35). Here, it is held, Paul is at his anti-feminist best.

Some wishing to avoid this conclusion, seek to explain the text in light of the synagogue worship out of which many of the Corinthians have come. Since women were segregated from men in the synagogue, the same practice, it is held, continued in the church. When the women, who were untaught in the synagogue, excercised their new-found Christian freedom by interrupting the service with questions, they shouted across the meeting to their husbands. Paul forbids this, they say, and demands that, "If there is anything they desire to know, let them ask their husbands at home" (14:35). While such a reconstruction explains this verse, it fails to account for the unequivocal command to silence in 14:34 and 35 which is grounded on the law in 14:34 and the word of God in 14:36. It also presupposes segregated worship which is unproven.

Others hold that in the immediate context the command to silence applies only to judging the prophetic utterances of others (14:32). This, however, would be a severe restriction on women and does not remove the offense of the passage.

A further view is that this paragraph was not originally written by Paul, but interpolated later by those wishing to conform the church to a more traditional, "Jewish" position.' Thus the surprising reference to the law (14:34) which sounds unPauline. We have, however, no manuscript evidence for the interpolation theory.

If we take the text as it stands, the major difficulty is its contradiction with I Corinthians 11:2-16 where women are expected to pray and prophesy. The answer that their praying and prophesying is not intended for public worship not only avoids the whole context of I Corinthians 11-14 which centers on public worship, but also makes the passage itself irrelevant. Prophecy must be spoken to the congregation for edification (I Corinthians 14:3-4); it is no private act.

Thus Paul is in the position of encouraging women to pray and prophesy and at the same time commanding them to be silent. This must force us to the conclusion that their silence is qualified. It relates only to questions which they are to reserve for their husbands at home (14:35).[10] They are not to disrupt the congregation. Their silence and subordination is based on the Old Testament, possibly Genesis 3:16, where God's judgement on Eve after the fall is that her husband "shall rule over you."

This silence, however, is qualified. Women are to pray and prophesy under the inspiration of the Spirit (I Corinthians 11:5). Here again is the breakthrough beyond the old orders of creation, the fall, and Jewish custom (see the full discussion of 11:2-16). This position must ultimately determine the order of the church, and Paul's references to women throughout his letters show that this is exactly the case.

While worship is to be ordered, and the Old Testament basis honored for congregational life, the final word is the gospel, the new age of the Holy Spirit and His gifts given to both men and women. In this light the command to women's silence is limited to specific abuses as the Corinthians emerged into the full light of God's new work taking them beyond the old orders.

If scripture interprets scripture, and if I Corinthians 14:33[a]-36 must be understood in context with I Corinthians 11:2-16, then this will be our final conclusion.

I Corinthians 16:19

19The churches of Asia send greetings, Aquila and Prisca, together with the church in their house, send you hearty greetings in the Lord.

Writing from Ephesus (16:8), Paul sends greetings from the Corinthian couple, Aquila and Prisca, who went with him to set up an advanced mission base (see Acts 18:1-27).

Together they have established a house church. The naming of Aquila first has no significance, as Paul reverses the order in Romans 16:3. Both are known and warmly tied to the Corinthians as they send "hearty greetings in the Lord."

In Conclusion

Paul operates on several fronts in I Corinthians. He opposes those libertines who, falsly interpreting his gospel of Christian freedom, would lead the church into moral and spiritual chaos. Against their rebellious and mystical freedom, Paul calls the church to maintain proper order and moral integrity, not offending its members or the watching world. Women are to remain veiled in public, and silent in worship. The man living in incest is to be cast out.

At the same time, Paul opposes those legalists who would determine the life of the church by custom and the Old Testament revelation. A new age has dawned - the age of the Spirit. We are now acceptable before God through the "foolish" cross which strips us of all pretention, pride and peformance (I Corinthians 1:17ff).

Since men and women are both justified by faith, they are to live out their life in Christ in a new relationship of freedom and dignity. This means that throughout I Corinthians 7 Paul deals with men and women equally in marital responsibility. Here at the very heart of their identity as expressed in the sexual encounter there is to be mutuality. Both marriage partners rule over each other's bodies.

Moreover, while the external order of women veiled and silent in worship is formally maintained, the internal order is radically changed. Wives are to express their dependence upon their husbands and proper place in the hierarchical structure of society, while at the same time in response to the Spirit they are free to transcend that society and participate with men in the spiritual life of the church through prayer and prophecy.

Here then is the heart of the churches' life because here is the heart of the gospel. Men and women are saved by faith in Christ alone. In marriage they are to love each other in mutuality. Gifted by the Spirit, they are both responsible to exercise their gifts to build up the congregation.

The hierarchical structure is revalued as the gospel brings us equally to God and as the Spirit gifts us equally for each other. Here is the new life for the new community living in the new age of God's redemption.

II CORINTHIANS

Introduction

Paul's second letter to the Corinthians contains many moods: warm entreaty, loving acceptance, bold confrontation, pointed rejoinder. Distinct issues and subjects are held together by the Apostle's unreserved self-giving and constant reference to Christ.[1]

The first seven chapters reveal Paul at his emotional and theological best. In the context of warm-heartedness, the Apostle defends his travel plans which appeared to vacillate and calls the church to forgive the man who caused him pain in his previous visit to Corinth (1:15-2:11).

Reflecting on the upsetting confrontation now past and perhaps anticipating the challenge of the fake apostles to be dealt with in chapters 10-13, Paul then interjects a long exposition of his new covenant ministry in the midst of news about himself (chapters 3-6). This ministry is contrasted with the old, Mosaic dispensation of the law and the external, passing, earthly form of this age which stands under the sign of death. In the context of suffering and persecution, Paul declares the gospel of the glory of Christ (4:4), and offers himself as a servant to the church and to the world (4:5). In his body the life of Jesus is manifested and his inner man is renewed daily as he walks by faith. From the vantage point of the new creation, Paul preaches the message that "God was in Christ reconciling the world to himself" (5:19), and he demonstrates the truth of the gospel in a life-style consistent with it (6:3-10).

After concluding remarks about himself and Titus in chapter 7, the Apostle then turns to the collection of an offering for the saints in Jerusalem (chapters 8-9; see also Romans 15:25-27). He calls upon the Corinthians to complete their giving started a year before (8:10), and makes plans for its reception.

This is then followed by Paul's defense of both the church and himself against "false apostles" who would undermine his ministry (chapters 10-13).

These missionaries claim Jewish credentials (11:22), commend themselves to the church (10:12), preach another Jesus in another spirit (11:4), and boast of their mission comparing themselves with Paul (11:12). They are deceitful and judged to be servants of Satan (11:14-15). The Corinthians easily capitulate to them (11:20).

Over and against these perverters Paul displays his ministry. He founded the church, betrothing it to Christ (11:2) and thus has authority to build up the Corinthians (10:8). Furthermore, Paul preached the gospel free of charge to them (11:7), and now displays his weaknesses and sufferings through which the power of Christ has been manifested (11:23-29; 12:1-13).

The historical events reflected in the letter include a painful visit to deal with opposition to Paul within the church (2:1ff), a planned return which was replaced by a strong letter (1:15-2:4; 7:8), and the subsequent reunion of Paul and Titus in Macedonia (7:5-7). From there Titus will go back to Corinth (8:16-17), along with other brethren and be followed by Paul himself (9:3-5).

It is in the context of personal issues, conflicts with "false apostles" and the exposition of his pastoral ministry that Paul makes reference to women in the church.

II Corinthians 11:1-3
¹I wish you would bear with me in a little foolishness. Do bear with me! ²I feel a divine jealousy for you, for I betrothed

you to Christ to present you as a pure bride to her one husband. *³But I am afraid that as the serpent deceived Eve by his cunning, your thoughts will be led astray from a sincere and pure devotion to Chrst.*

In the immediate context Paul is defending himself against the "superlative apostles" who would undercut his ministry. His position in contrast to them is primary in the church because it is he who introduced the Corinthians to Christ. Thus he does not boast in other's labors as these bogus missionaries do (10:13-18).

His foolishness in 11:1 is revealed by his "boasting" in his ministry. It is foolish because the Corinthians are to boast in the Lord (10:17), but it is necessary as a defense against his opponents who impress the church by boasting of their own accomplishments in a worldly way (11:16ff).

Paul's jealousy for the Corinthians is "divine" because he betrothed them not to himself but to Christ. The purpose of the betrothal was to present the church "as a pure bride to her one husband" (11:2). Here Paul employs the marriage metaphor to illustrate his calling and the Corinthian's conversion.

The Apostle functioned as the intermediary to unite the church to Christ. The union of the two is analogous to the union of husband and wife in Genesis 2:24 - they are to become "one flesh." The church is to be pure, that is, faithful to Christ. He is to be the one husband deserving absolute loyalty and allegiance. If the Corinthians are led away from Him they will be spiritual adulterers.

The church is to view itself as the "bride" of Christ. While "bride" may suggest submissiveness and receptivity, here Paul emphasizes that the bride is called to be "faithful" - it is her purity which is demanded (11:2). She is to have "one husband."

The "superlative apostles" would lead the church astray even as after the creation in Genesis 2 Adam and Eve were led astray in

Genesis 3. Thus Paul naturally follows the idea of the Corinthians' marriage to Christ with a warning based on Eve's deception. It is the serpent, however, and not Eve who is the tempter; the church is to guard against his "cunning." The false apostles represent the serpent and, as Satan "disguises himself as an angel of light" (11:14), so will they as his servants (11:15).

It is important to note that the whole church, male and female, is made analogous to Eve. Like Eve we are called to be faithful to Christ and at the same time are in danger of deception. It is Christ who fulfills Adam's spiritual destiny before the fall. Betrothed to Him by faith we are to live devotedly with Him in sincerity and purity (11:3). Our high calling is to live in a divine marriage union with Christ.

GALATIANS

Introduction

Galatians is written in the white-heat of theological and personal controversy. Paul's apostleship and message are under attack. False teachers have invaded the young Galatian churches demanding that Gentile converts be circumcised and keep the Old Testament law if they are to be true Christians (5:2-4; 6:12-13).

Not only is the gospel of justification by faith being subverted, but Paul's apostleship is also in dispute. His opponents claim that he cannot be a true apostle because he was not personally called by Christ (contrast 1:1). He is at most a secondary missionary, dependent upon the Jerusalem church (contrast 1:15-17).

Paul responds with a strong defense of his call by Christ and his independence from other apostles (chapters 1-2). His vocation and message have been given by revelation (1:11-12). It was not until three years after his conversion that he first went to Jerusalem to visit Peter and James (1:18-19). He did not return again until fourteen years later (2:1-10). Then the pillars of the church added nothing from the law to the simplicity of his gospel of salvation by faith alone. Endorsing his ministry, they extended the "right hand of fellowship" (2:9) and dispatched him to the Gentiles.

After this historical defense of his calling, Paul turns to the gospel itself (chapters 3-4). The Galatians received the Holy Spirit by hearing the message of Christ crucified and believing it "by faith" (3:1-5).

This message fulfills God's promise to Abraham and relieves us from the burden of the Mosaic law with its demand for moral perfection (3:6-12). Christ became a curse for us by bearing the demand of the law so that God's salvation blessing can now be freely given (3:13-14).

The law cannot save us; its design is to bring us to Christ. Only when we despair over our moral failure are we ready for a savior. Now all are accepted simply by faith on the basis of Christ's death for sin (3:26).

Turning from theology, Paul appeals to his personal relationship with the Galatians in 4:12ff pleading with them to remember their love for him. This is followed by an allegory about freedom and slavery based on Abraham and his sons (4:21-31).

Now Paul applies the gospel of freedom from the law to the Christian life (chapters 5-6). Rather than living in bondage, believers are to walk in the Spirit loving and serving each other. Christ will be real to them as they trust Him and care for each other.

This then is the major thrust of Galatians. The issue? Christ plus. The gospel is not Christ plus the law. The gospel is Christ *period*. It is in relationship to this gospel that we must understand women in the church.

Galatians 3:28

[28]*There is neither Jew nor Greek, there is neither slave nor free, there is neither male nor female; for you are all one in Christ Jesus.*

Paul concludes his exposition of the gospel with the announcement of our oneness in Christ. Since we are accepted by God not on the basis of the works of the law but on the basis of faith alone, there is no ground for competition, no differing value system to keep us from each other, no boasting possible.

We are one in our sin, one in deserving God's judgment and one in our salvation as God's free "yes" is given to us in Christ. We are all sons of God by faith (3:26). We are all baptized into Christ (3:27). The results of this are clear - the old legal divisions, the old distinctions, the old separations are broken down.

So Paul begins, "There is neither Jew nor Greek...." In other words, the racial barriers evidenced in the Old Testament law have been abolished. God called Abraham not simply to bless Israel, but to bless all nations (Genesis 12:1ff). Now, in the time of fulfillment, in the new age of the Spirit, His purpose is accomplished as Jew and Gentile come together in the one body of Christ. Thus it is necessary that Jew and Gentile live together and eat together (see 2:11ff), so that the gospel will be believed. If the law has been lifted, if Christ has taken the curse (3:13), then we must demonstrate this reality by our unity. Here is the end of racial distinctions and racism. The church is to be that people who live together not because of cultural or sociological compatibility but because of Christ.

Paul continues, "There is neither slave nor free...." Not only are racial barriers abolished, social and economic barriers have gone with them. Slaves were legally considered property in the Roman Empire. They were tallied along with chariots, horses, and household items. In the church not only were they revalued as persons, but they were also seen as the equals of free citizens in Christ. While the structure of slavery was continued in the world, the value system upon which it was based was destroyed in the church. Thus the runaway slave Onesimus was to be welcomed home as a brother by his master (Philemon 16). Now it was only a matter of time until the institution of slavery itself would be destroyed by the truth of the gospel. Again, we see that there is no barrier that Christ will not overcome. If reconciliation has been accomplished, it must be visualized in the life-style of the church. Christ's love will draw diverse people from different classes together.

Now Paul concludes, "there is neither male nor female (literally 'male and female' - see Genesis 1:27[1]); for you are all one in Christ Jesus." As the racial and social barriers are broken down, so also are the sexual distinctions due to the creation of "male and female." Here is Paul's radical step beyond the old order. Redemption does not merely restore God's intention in creation. Redemption brings into being a whole new world, a whole new order.

Male dominance, egotism, patriarchal power and preferential priority is at an end. No longer can Genesis 2-3 be employed to reduce woman to an inferior position or state. If redemption is real the warfare between the sexes is over. At the same time, female seduction, manipulation, and domineering is also over, "for you are all one in Christ Jesus."

Furthermore, the life-style of the church must be consistent with the gospel of the church. Proclamation must result in demonstration. If we are all justified by faith, then the radical revaluing of Jew and Greek, slave and free and male and female will be seen as all live together in the church of Christ. While the formal structures of the world will not necessarily change immediately, the values are radically changed and a new life-style will emerge among the people of God consistent with the gospel of God's free grace. We conclude that the old barriers are broken as Christ makes all things new.

Galatians 4:4-5

[4]But when the time had fully come, God sent forth his Son, born of woman, born under the law, [5]to redeem those who were under the law, so that we might receive adoption as sons.

At the climax to his theological section, Paul offers an explanation for his statement that now we are Abraham's offspring, "heirs according to the promise" (3:29).

Prior to Christ's coming, although Go
we were like children under "guardians and
is no better than a slave until the date for his
so we were in bondage to the "elemental spirits
(4:3). Now, however, all has changed.

The time has fully come because Christ has come fulfilling God's promise to us (4:4). God has sent forth His Son from eternity into time, from the divine heart to human need. God's Son, moreover, has been "born of woman" (4:4). There could be no stronger statement than this for the full humanity of Christ. He came from the Father, not simply as the divine Son untouched by our humanity. He was not an angelic mirage or ghost. He was "born of woman"; he entered this world in a fully human way - and by implication, in the weakness of an infant, in the humility of a small child.

The phrase "born of woman" does not necessarily refer to the virgin birth. The Apostle is not stressing the miracle of Christ's birth, but its human reality. The deity of Christ is held in the previous phrase, "God sent forth His Son." The humanity of Christ is then expressed in "born of woman" and the Jewishness of Christ is represented in "born under the law" (4:4).

The purpose of Christ's coming appears in 4:5. He has come to redeem us from the curse of the law (see 3:13), and to restore us to God's family, "so that we might receive adoption as sons."

In the phrase, "born of woman," the dignity of humanity, womanhood and motherhood is enshrined. God's Son became a human being - we are to rejoice in our creaturehood sanctified by Christ. God's Son came through a woman - women are to rejoice in the honor of bearing the Messiah. God's Son came through a mother - mothers are to rejoice that birth is holy - that as God's Son was born into our world so the birth process is God's chosen way to enter our flesh and blood.

Galatians 4:21-31

[21] *Tell me, you who desire to be under law, do you not hear the law?* [22] *For it is written that Abraham had two sons, one by a slave and one by a free woman.* [23] *But the son of the slave was born according to the flesh, the son of the free woman through promise.* [24] *Now this is an allegory: these women are two covenants. One is from Mount Sinai, bearing children for slavery; she is Hagar.* [25] *Now Hagar is Mount Sinai in Arabia; she corresponds to the present Jerusalem, for she is in slavery with her children.* [26] *But the Jerusalem above is free, and she is our mother.* [27] *For it is written, "Rejoice, O barren one that dost not bear; break forth and shout, thou who art not in travail; for the desolate hath more children than she who hath a husband."* [28] *Now we, brethren, like Isaac, are children of promise.* [29] *But as at that time he who was born according to the flesh persecuted him who was born according to the Spirit so it is now.* [30] *But what does the scripture say? "Cast out the slave and her son; for the son of the slave shall not inherit with the son of the free woman."* [31] *So, brethren, we are not children of the slave but of the free woman.*

Continuing his attack on the legalists, Paul abruptly changes from personal entreaty (4:12-20) to a lengthy allegory based on Abraham's two mates and their two sons. It is as if the Apostle says to his Jewish-Christian opponents - "all right, if you want to use legal arguments from the Old Testament and rabbinic exegesis, I can do the same." He then proceeds to defeat them at their own game by showing that there are two lines of inheritance from Abraham, the father of the Jewish people. The first line is represented in his son Ishmael who was born of Sarah's slave Hagar (Genesis 16:1ff). This was a "fleshly" birth representing Abraham's trust in his own means, and the old covenant of the law given from Sinai, seen now in the earthly Jerusalem which is "in slavery with her children" (4:25). The second line is represented in his son

Isaac who was born by Sarah as a child of God's promise (Genesis 21:1ff). This was a spiritual birth, Sarah being a free woman receiving God's grace. She also represents the "Jerusalem above," heaven itself, which is free and we who believe in Christ are, "like Isaac...children of promise" (4:28).

While those born of the Spirit are persecuted today, as was Isaac by Ishmael, we will inherit God's future because we are Sarah's children: children of freedom, children of promise, children of the Spirit.

We see here Paul's liberty in applying the Old Testament to the church. While he does not shy away from allegory, neither does he allow it to run wild. His presentation is based on Abraham's two sons and is soundly anchored in the history of God's call and promise to Abraham as the man of faith and the line of grace given through Isaac (see 3:6-9). Thus theology and history control his allegory.

Also, Paul uses two women, Hagar and Sarah, as the sources for life in the flesh and life in the Spirit. They symbolize slavery and freedom, the Jerusalem below and above.

The Jerusalem above, analagous to Sarah, is described as "our mother" (4:26), and we are children "of the free woman" (4:31), namely Sarah, when we receive the gospel. Thus while we are sons of Abraham by faith (3:7, 29), we are also sons and daughters of Sarah (4:31).

What we learn from this passage is that Paul is free to use feminine illustrations and language to describe Christians. He is not bound simply to employing male forms. Moreover, he is comfortable describing believers as coming from their mother, the heavenly spiritual Jerusalem, and Sarah, the free woman who represents the gospel.

Not only this, Paul also has a firm sense of history. God's promise comes through Abraham *and Sarah* to us. If Abraham is our father by his faith and by his becoming the object of God's gracious work thoughout history, then Sarah is our mother. Together Abraham and Sarah carry on the line of God's purpose now fulfilled in Christ.

Not only does Paul use Sarah in a non-sexist way, he also offers her as an identity model for the Christian. Consider yourself a child of Sarah when you receive the gospel of freedom. Our Old Testament identity is held by both a man and a woman through whom God began the fulfillment of His promise to mankind.

Finally, to be a Christian is to be "born according to the Spirit" (4:29). The birth metaphor presupposes a woman as the means of that birth. Thus a basic New Testament image for conversion has a feminine source. The heavenly Jerusalem and Sarah are our mothers when we enter God's family.

In Galatians we see the balance of Paul. Both Abraham and Sarah bear the gospel to us. We belong to them both. In Christ both become the necessary means and models for our new life. To belong to Christ means that we are children of Abraham and children of Sarah. Here is our family identity!

In Conclusion

Paul announces the gospel of liberation from the curse and bondage of the law. With that liberation comes an end to the old divisions, including "male and female." Now is the new creation where redemption is lived out in a whole new life-style. This radical gospel, elevating women to a position of equality before God is underscored as Christ is "born of woman" sanctifying both our humanity and motherhood. This radical gospel also lets us see ourselves as sons and daughters of Sarah, born again into the heavenly Jerusalem, our mother. Now our Christian identity does not deny created distinctions but it both fulfills them and transcends them as we claim the totality of what God has given us: sons and daughters of Sarah, all one in Christ Jesus.

EPHESIANS

Introduction

The thesis of Ephesians, one of Paul's most theological letters, is that while sin divides, Christ unites. Into a disordered cosmos of rebellion and strife, Christ has come accomplishing redemption in His cross and achieving rulership over all things in His resurrection and ascension (1:20-23). Now as Lord of the universe, He is head of His body the church, where former Jews and Gentiles have become new people and are living out their life together (2:11-15).

God's plan is to unite all things in Christ (1:10). Purposed from eternity (1:4), and executed in history (1:7), this plan is now being proclaimed to the world by Paul (3:7-8).

Having laid this foundation (chapters 1-3), the Apostle calls upon us to live out the meaning of the union of all things in Christ (chapters 4-6). As always, for Paul the indicative is followed by the imperative.

Grounded then in Christ's making peace through His cross, believers are to celebrate their oneness in their calling to be together (4:1ff). This will be accomplished through the gifted community of the church growing up into Christ as each speaks the truth to the other (4:15). This community functions through forgiveness (4:32), love (5:2), thanksgiving (5:4) and worship (5:19).

As the church realizes the oneness of Christ's body and grows in it, this will then be reflected in marriage relationships between husbands and wives (5:21-33), in family relationships between parents and children (6:1-4), and in economic relationships between slaves and masters (6:5-9). The proclamation of all things united in Christ will be credible through the demonstration of Christians living in accordance with the truth of the gospel.

These giant themes are addressed by Paul to unknown Gentile converts who have heard of him but have not seen him (3:2). Likewise, he has only heard of them (1:15). Since the phrase "in Ephesus" (1:1) is missing in many of our best Greek manuscripts, "Ephesians" is probably a circular letter written to several congregations to establish them in a true knowledge of the gospel. It is in the context of "unity in Christ" then that we need to view what Paul says about women in the church.

Ephesians 5:21-33

21Be subject to one another out of reverence for Christ. 22Wives, be subject to your husbands, as to the Lord. 23For the husband is the head of the wife as Christ is the head of the church, his body, and is himself its Savior. 24As the church is subject to Christ, so let wives also be subject in everything to their husbands. 25Husbands, love your wives, as Christ loved the church and gave himself up for her, 26that he might sanctify her, having cleansed her by the washing of water with the word, 27that he might present the church to himself in splendor, without spot or wrinkle or any such thing, that she might be holy and without blemish. 28Even so husbands should love their wives as their own bodies. He who loves his wife loves himself. 29For no man ever hates his own flesh, but nourishes and cherishes it, as Christ does the church. 30because we are members of his body. 31For this reason a man shall leave his father and mother and be joined to his wife, and the two shall become one." 32This is a great mystery, and I take it to mean Christ and the church; 33however, let each one of you love his wife as himself, and let the wife see that she respects her husband.

Paul's exhortation to husbands and wives presupposes the exhortation to the church contained in 4:1-5:20. Only when the church is becoming what God intended it to be will marriage be what God intended it to be. In other words, the church is not to depend upon the Christian home for its life, but rather the Christian home is to depend upon the church for its life. The quality of the family, and especially the relationship between husbands and wives, will mirror the quality of the congregation.

The Apostle begins with a call for the mutual subordination of husbands and wives: "Be subject to one another out of reverence for Christ" (5:21). Grammatically this connects Paul's exhortation to worship in 5:18-20 with his teaching on marriage starting in 5:22. Marriage will be Christian only as *both partners* submit themselves to each other. This mutual subordination is reflected in Paul's instruction on the quality of Christian community throughout Ephesians: "Let everyone speak the truth with his neighbor, for we are members one of another" (4:25); "Be kind to one another, tenderhearted, forgiving one another, as God in Christ forgave you." (4:32); "Walk in love as Christ loved us and gave Himself up for us...." (5:2). Thus marriage is to reflect the renewed interpersonal relationships of the Christian community. Its presupposition is redeemed, healed, growing partners who are subject to Christ, to the body of Christ and to each other as Christians. We must note at this point that Paul begins with no doctrine of male superiority or dominance.

Mutual subordination is then expressed by wives in their being subject to their husbands "as to the Lord" (5:22). Their subjection is never unqualified: it is their subjection to Christ which is to define and determine their subjection to their husbands. Since Christ is the standard, the criterion for their subjection, it is never to be in violation of truth, morality or especially, in violation of the gospel. Christ's lordship over wives will never allow them to be subject to the sin or selfishness or the arbitrary will of their husbands. Their prior responsibility to their husbands is to speak "the truth in love" (4:15) as Christians. Thus they help their husbands grow up into "the measure of the stature of the fullness of Christ...." (4:13).

The subjection of wives in the Lord is predicated upon husbands being "the head of the wife as Christ is the head of the church, His body, and is Himself its Savior." Headship here denotes the source of life and growth rather than mere authority (see 4:15-16). Christ's headship is seen in His giving Himself to save the church. He is its servant. So husbands are to express their headship by giving themselves for their wives (see 5:25-30).

Paul continues addressing wives by asking them to be "subject in everything to their husbands," "as the church is subject to Christ." Again their submission is not unqualified. Christ is the model, the example. As husbands give themselves to their wives, their wives are to be subject to their giving husbands.

Wives, rather than living independent, arrogant, self-realized lives are to live in dependence upon their husbands. They are to receive life from them, as they are served by them (see below). Paul neither teaches self-sufficiency nor does he teach meek submission. He does teach mature dependency and self realization for wives only in relationship to Christ and the intimate other - their husbands. Here is, in Martin Buber's words, "dialogical" life.

At the same time, husbands express their mutual subjection to their wives by loving them "as Christ loved the church and gave Himself up for her...." (5:25). The goal of Christ's sacrifice was to sanctify the church, cleansing her, to present the church to Himself as a glorious, holy bride (5:26-27). Thus husbands are to so love their wives, even as they love their own bodies and themselves (5:28) with the same goal before them.

Now the subjection of wives to their husbands becomes clear. They are to be in subjection to the love *(agape)* given to them by their husbands. This love will be the very love of Christ, that is, it will be self-less and self-sacrificing, coming from the divine heart. This love will have as its goal not the selfish meeting of the husbands' needs, but the maturity, and holiness ("wholeness") of their wives.

The key word is the verb "give" (5:25). Wives are to submit to the giving of their husbands. Husbands are to be the head of their wives as they give themselves to and for their wives. Here is no tyranny. Here is no male domination. Here is service. Here is foot washing (John 13:1-5; 12-14). Here is the mind (attitude) of Christ which renounces its rights to live humbly in the world (Philippians 2:5-11).

Not only are husbands to love their wives as Christ loved the church, but also they are to love as they love themselves (5:28-30). Paul speaks of husbands nourishing and cherishing their own bodies as Christ does the church. This again is to be the quality of love and care to which wives submit.

The ground for all of this is that the command of Genesis 2:24, the union of husband and wife in the one flesh, is now fulfilled redemptively in the union of Christ and the church (5:31-32). Since we are members of His body, united to Christ, this must manifest itself in the marriage relationship. Apart from Christ and the church the union of marriage in "one flesh" will never be possible. Only as we are united to Christ can we be united to each other. The ordinance of marriage can now only be fulfilled in Christ. He is the presupposition for the marriage union, and this union is to reflect the union of the church to Christ. Love and respect will be its fruit (5:33).[1]

What can we say then in conclusion to this passage?

1. Christian marriage presupposes and mirrors the functioning Christian community.

2. Christian marriage is always Christologically defined - that is, the relationship between husbands and wives is always determined by Jesus Christ and the church.

3. Christian marriage is egalitarian and a partnership in that husbands and wives are to live in mutual submission to Christ and to each other.

4. Wives express their submission by surrendering themselves to the love of Christ given them through their husbands.

5. Husbands express their submission by loving their wives as Christ loved the church and gave Himself for her.

6. Husbands' love for their wives is to be no less than their love for themselves. The standard again, is the love of Christ for His body, the church.

7. Marriage is to reflect the union of man and woman in the "one flesh" which is now realized first in the spiritual union of Christ and the church and then reflected in the marriage union.

In conclusion, while Paul maintains the traditional hierarchical structure of the submission of wives to their husbands he modifies it by mutual submission and changes the content. Christ is the standard and model. It is the love of Christ and the body of Christ which are to determine the context and quality of marriage. Christian marriage, rather than demeaning the wife, is to be her liberation and fulfillment in that she is cared for by the very love of Christ given through her husband. Christian marriage is also a call to the husband to throw himself upon the grace of Christ. Only here will he receive the strength to be Christ to his wife and to fulfill God's intention to make him and his wife one.

Ephesians 6:1-3

¹Children, obey your parents in the Lord, for this is right.
²"Honor your father and mother" (this is the first

commandment with a promise), [3]*"that it may be well with you and that you may live long on the earth."*

Paul moves from the Christian community, to husbands and wives, to parents and children. The obedience of children to parents presupposes all that has gone before.

Children are to obey their parents "in the Lord" (6:1). That is, they are to obey their parents not with unqualified submission, but as their parents live in the Lord and model the love of Christ for the church and the union of Christ with the church (5:21-33).

By parents the Apostle means husbands and wives. This becomes explicit in the quotation from Exodus 20:12 and Deuteronomy 5:16. Children are to honor their fathers and mothers. The task of discipline is intrusted primarily to fathers to bring their children "up in the discipline and instruction of the Lord" (6:4). Obedience and honor, however, are to be given to mothers as well as fathers (6:1-2). The standard at all times is "in the Lord." Christ is the test for obedience and honor. Thus obedience is neither absolute nor arbitrary. The child must always appeal beyond his or her parent to the Lord.

For our discussion it is important to note that obedience "in the Lord" is due mothers as well as fathers. Honor also is for both, although discipline and the instruction of the Lord are primarily the task of fathers (6:4). Since the husband is to receive the love of Christ for his wife, so he is to receive the instruction of Christ for his child. This does not, however, demean or bypass the wife. She too requires obedience and honor "in the Lord" (6:1-2), which presupposes that she bears authority with her children. Both parents are responsible for their families but fathers are especially responsible for discipline. This demand, rather than absolving women from such a task (which is clearly accepted in 6:1), forces men to accept similar responsibility.

In Conclusion

God's plan to unite all things in Christ is manifested in the redeemed community of the church. The home then is an extension of that community. There in mutual submission, Christians are to live together: husbands loving as Christ loved, wives submitting "in the Lord." Such parents are also to discipline and instruct their obedient children "in the Lord." Authority is exercised in love as Christ is the model and motive for all things.

PHILIPPIANS

Introduction

Philippians calls us to journey into the joy of Christ. In the midst of imprisonment and facing an unknown future, Paul rejoices in the Lord (3:1) and summons his church to a similar joy.

Grateful for a gift of money carried to him from Philippi by Epaphroditus (2:25-30; 4:10-20), the Apostle writes a warm personal response not only to receipt the offering, but also to address pressing issues in the church. These include the persecution by the state (1:29-30), a personal conflict between two women, Euodia and Syntyche (4:2-3), which is threatening the unity of the church (2:1-11), and false teaching which would seduce the believers away from their faithfulness to Christ. This heresy includes legalism, perfectionism and materialism (3:2-21).

At every point Paul calls the church back to Christ. In Him the Philippians have everything - why turn away from His supremacy and adequacy?

Against persecution the Apostle writes, "For me to live is Christ and to die is gain" (1:21). To heal division he calls the church to the mind (attitude) of Christ who renounced His rights to be humbled in the world (2:5ff). To combat false teachers Paul offers his own testimony (3:1ff). Over and against the legalism of Judaism, he extols the joy and freedom of Christ. Over and against those who claim perfection, he presses on to the goal of Christ (3:14). Over and against this world, he holds citizenship in heaven and focuses the Philippians on the Christ who is to come (3:20ff).

In sum, Paul's answer for every issue is Christ and Christ alone. As he concludes, "I have learned in whatever state I am, to be content. I know how to be abased, and I know how to abound; in any and all circumstances I have learned the secret of facing plenty and hunger, abundance and want. I can do all things in Him who strengthens me" (4:11-13). From the center which is Christ; His supremacy, His sufficiency, His humility, we look again at the question of women in the church.

Philippians 4:2-3

²*I entreat Euodia and I entreat Syntyche to agree in the Lord.* ³*And I ask you also, true yokefellow, help these women, for they have labored side by side with me in the gospel together with Clement and the rest of my fellow workers, whose names are in the book of life.*

As Paul comes to the conclusion of his letter he calls upon two women to be reconciled. The repetition of the verb, "I entreat," "I entreat," is highly emphatic.

The specific reference to division here illumines the Apostle's reason for the great Christological passage in 2:1-11. Paul calls the Philippians to renounce selfishness and conceit (2:3) and to have the mind of Christ (2:5ff) because Euodia and Syntyche are not getting along. Their conflict is endangering the unity of the church. Not only will this destroy God's work in Philippi, but disunity also belies the gospel. How will the world believe that Christ has reconciled us to the Father and to each other if we cannot live together? Thus the stakes are high as Paul calls these women back to each other.

The passage itself is simple. "True yokefellow" is asked to mediate the conflict. At the same time, Paul highly commends these women, expressing respect and affection for them. Several important points emerge.

Firstly, Euodia and Syntyche are in such positions of leadership in the church in Philippi that they can endanger its unity. They are not simply spending their time doing behind the scenes domestic tasks for the congregation. Paul never challenges their position; he both assumes it and accepts it. What he does confront is their attitudes toward each other as they carry out their responsibilities.

Secondly, their conflict appears not to be doctrinal but personal. If these women were engaged in theological controversy, Paul would correct and rebuke them (compare Galatians 1). His approach based on 2:1-11 is to humble them and to call them again to Christ. Christ is to be their model for service and obedience and they are to agree "in the Lord" (4:2).

Thirdly, Paul commends Euodia and Syntyche using the strongest possible terms. He writes, "they have labored side by side with me (or "fought beside me") in the gospel" (4:3). The compound verb "labored side by side" denotes unity in sharing a common task. These women did not serve under Paul or behind Paul or below Paul; they served *beside* Paul. They were equal with him in a common ministry. Notice too that they labored or battled together "in the gospel." Again, it is clear that Euodia and Syntyche shared in the proclamation of the faith, in ministering the gospel itself and not simply in menial tasks. It is their very position in the ministry with Paul and in the gospel which has made them able to destroy the unity of the Philippians.

Furthermore, Paul identifies these women not only with himself but also with another male, Clement and "the rest of my fellow workers" (4:3). Thus Euodia and Syntyche are called "fellow workers" or "co-workers," again standing beside Paul and others in the ministry of the gospel. As another woman, Prisca, was called a fellow worker in Romans 16:3, so Euodia and Syntyche share a similar designation here. Paul elsewhere applies the same title to Aquila (Romans 16:3), Urbanus (Romans 16:9),

Timothy (Romans 16:21; I Thessalonians 3:2), Mark, Aristarchus, Demas, Luke (Philemon 24), and Epaphroditus (Philippians 2:25). Thus it becomes clear that both men and women held essential positions of ministry in the gospel with Paul.

The joy of the Lord will only be full if the church is one, embracing together the mind of Christ which is the Lord's already present gift (2:5). For this reason, Paul summons Euodia and Syntyche to come together and asks a brother to intercede between them.

COLOSSIANS

Introduction

Colossians declares the adequacy and supremacy of Christ. He is both the agent of creation (1:16) and the agent of redemption (1:18-20). He is the goal toward which everything moves. He holds everything together (1:16-17). In Him all the fulness of God was pleased to dwell (1:19) and in Him the Colossians have come to fulness of life (2:10).

Paul presents this powerful picture of Christ in chapter 1 to prepare for his warning against a "counter movement" in chapter 2 which would compromise the finality of Christ. The Apostle's strategy is clear: the best defense is a good offense. Once the church's vision is filled with Christ the false alternatives will pale into insignificance.

The "counter movement" in Colossae consists of a deceitful philosophy (2:8) combined with a rigorous legalism (2:16-19). The philosophy appears to be a cosmological system concerning the stars and their angelic rulers ("the elemental spirits of the universe," 2:8,20). It includes the worship of angels and visions (2:18). Over and against these lesser astrological authorities stands Christ "who is the head of all rule and authority" (2:10). The stars are dependent upon Him. Moreover, the evil principalities and powers have been disarmed through the cross of Christ (2:15). The Christian now need have no fear of them.

Not only have the Colossians been delivered from a fallen universe, they have also been delivered from a false ritualism and legalism designed to achieve final salvation. The old Jewish ceremonies were merely a shadow of that which has been revealed completely in Christ (2:16-17). The old legal requirements of the law and the mortification of the flesh are of no value to Christians who have died to the old world in Christ and who have been raised into a new life in the Spirit (2:20-23).

Having established his thesis for the supremacy of Christ (chapters 1-2), Paul then shows how Christ's sovereignty is to be lived out in a new quality of community life under His lordship (chapters 3-4). The old sinful life is to be surrendered (3:5-9); the new life in Christ of truth, forgiveness, love and peace is to be embraced (3:10-17). Since Christ "is all, and in all" this must be seen in the church and applied to the world.

As in Ephesians, after Paul expounds the nature of Christian community, he turns to its extension in the family (3:18-21) and society (3:22-4:1). A redeemed body of people will begin to redeem the structures of society. We will make a difference because we are different.

Colossians is written to a congregation unknown to Paul personally. The church was established by Epaphras who is credentialed and commended by the Apostle (1:3-8, 4:12-13). Paul accepts the wider responsibility for his extended ministry by responding to the need of the Colossians to be presented "mature in Christ" (1:28).

Colossians 3:18-19

[18]*Wives, be subject to your husbands, as is fitting in the Lord.* [19]*Husbands, love your wives and do not be harsh with them.*

In a vein similar to Ephesians 5:21-33, Paul calls upon wives to submit themselves to their husbands. Lacking is the call to mutual submission as in Ephesians 5:21, which makes the exhortation somewhat harsh. At the same time, there is no essential difference in content. The submission of wives is not unqualified, it is "as is fitting in the Lord" (3:18). This presupposes the mutual Christian responsibility of both partners first to behave toward each other as Christians in the body of Christ (3:1-17). As they are growing in truth, forgiveness, love, and peace, then wives are to be submissive only in consistency with their life "in the Lord." It is Christ who is the standard, motivation and ruler of their submission. That of their husbands which is not "fitting in the Lord" cannot and must not be the object of their submission.

This becomes immediately clear in 3:19: "Husbands, love your wives, and do not be harsh with them." The object of the wives' submission is the self-sacrificing, self-giving love of their husbands. This love (*agape*) only comes from God (I Thessalonians 4:9), and seeks not its own good, but that of the other. Thus wives are to submit themselves to the self-giving love of their husbands which seeks their fulfillment. In the context of this kind of love all harshness or bitterness (a reflection of selfishness) is ruled out (3:19). Tenderness and sensitivity are the order of the day. As Paul writes in 3:12-13, "Put on then, as God's chosen ones, holy and beloved, compassion, kindness, lowliness, meekness and patience, forbearing one another and, if one has a complaint against another, forgiving each other; as the Lord has forgiven you, so you also must forgive." It is the quality of relationships in the Christian community which must be reflected in Christian marriage. Male egotism and macho spirit is excluded by the love of Christ.

Colossians 3:20

[20]Children, obey your parents in everything, for this pleases the Lord.

Here is the fifth commandment (Exodus 20:12) paraphrased and made Christocentric. Children are to honor their parents by obedience (compare Ephesians 6:1-3). We must remember that the parents presupposed here, however, are Christians living together in the body of Christ, reflecting the character of Christ.

Thus obedience is qualified by the whole context of the letter. The goal is not simply pleasing parents, it is pleasing the Lord, or literally, "this is pleasing in the Lord." Obedience is never outside of Christ. As for wives and husbands, so for children - Christ is the context, standard and Lord of the family.

By "parents" Paul calls for the obedience of children to both fathers and mothers without distinction.

Colossians 4:15

15Give my greetings to the brethren at Laodicea, and to Nympha and the church in her house.

Along with the brethren in Laodicea, Nympha is especially singled out for a greeting from Paul. She is personally known to him, and exercises her hospitality to believers by welcoming them into her home. The "house church" is also mentioned of Prisca and Aquila (Romans 16:3-5) and Philemon (Philemon 2). Paul easily greets this lady and honors her especially by naming her alone among the Laodiceans. That women exercised special gifts and influence in the church and Paul's life is reflected in this verse.

I THESSALONIANS

Introduction

Paul writes this letter to a young church from which he was abruptly separated while engaged in his missionary task (2:17). Having been thwarted from completing his grounding of these new converts in their faith, the Apostle went on to Athens fearing for their survival (3:1ff). Unable to relax his concern, Paul dispatched Timothy back to Thessalonica to see if the church had stood under continuing persecution. Now Timothy has returned with the good news of the Thessalonians' faith and love (3:6), and some unanswered questions for Paul concerning moral issues and those who have died before the Lord's return (4:2-8; 4:13-5:11).

The Apostle therefore writes I Thessalonians to continue his grounding of the church in its new faith. In the letter he pursues his teaching task by reminding the believers of his example in evangelism and edification (chapters 1-2) and giving them exhortation again about the distinctives of the Christian life (chapters 4-5). In this context he deals with the dead in Christ and the coming of the Lord (4:13ff).

Paul presents his example before the church and commends the Thessalonians for their imitation of himself (1:6), not because he is the supreme egotist, but because he is a good teacher. Paul knows that new converts will learn how to live the Christian life by imitating a real Christian. Paul also ministers out of a traveling community of helpers (1:1) and this becomes a model for the Thessalonians' community in Christ. Thus he continually speaks in the plural (i.e. "we").

After recalling his own example and praying for the church, Paul presents again the formal teaching and exhortation previously given (4:1-2). What makes the Christian life unique? The Apostle responds by calling the Thessalonians to sexual purity (4:3-8), love (4:9-10), work (4:11-12), and hope (4:13-5:11). The letter concludes with general exhortation (5:12-28).

I Thessalonians 2:7-8

7But we were gentle among you, like a nurse taking care of her children. 8So, being affectionately desirous of you, we were ready to share with you not only the gospel of God but also our own selves, because you had become very dear to us.

After his primary evangelistic preaching (2:1-6), Paul engaged in nurturing and establishing his new converts (2:7-12). As he reflects upon this task he employs two images to describe his care for them, that of a nurse or mother (2:7) and that of a father (2:11).

Paul begins by expressing his unconditional love and care for the Thessalonians. To do this he pictures himself as a nurse or mother "taking care of her children" (2:7). The phrase can be literally translated, "holding her children against her breast." Here is an image of tenderness, warmth, care, protection, support and nourishment. Paul sees his responsibility to his converts first as a "feminine" one - he is to love them with a mother's love.

This becomes clear in 2:8 where Paul uses highly emotional language to express his commitment to the church. "So, being affectionately desirous of you, we were ready to share...our own selves, because you had become very dear (beloved) to us." Paul gave both the gospel and himself to the Thessalonians. He treated them as his own children and he loved them extravagantly.

From this we learn that Paul is free to express himself as a mother to her children. Paul has no need to defend a stereotyped "male" image. When proper, Paul identifies himself with mother-like qualities.

Furthermore, a mother's love is one of the best pictures of the gospel and the nurturing of the Christian community. Every new believer deserves and needs a mother in the faith - a human means of grace, acceptance, support and care.

This image also expresses the radical commitment necessary to help new Christians grow. Here is a total concern for their welfare. As Paul says, "We were ready to share with you...our own selves...." (2:8).

Paul is first a mother (2:7) and then a father (2:11). Only when Christians are loved unconditionally like a mother can they be exhorted properly like a father. Each believer needs both - but growth begins with a mother's love. This is not optional. It is a matter of spiritual life and health.

I Thessalonians 4:3-8

³For this is the will of God, your sanctification: that you abstain from immorality; ⁴that each one of you know how to take a wife for himself in holiness and honor, ⁵not in the passion of lust like heathen who do not know God; ⁶that no man transgress, and wrong his brother in this matter, because the Lord is an avenger in all these things, as we solemnly forewarned you. ⁷For God has not called us for uncleanness, but in holiness. ⁸Therefore whoever disregards this, disregards not man but God, who gives his Holy Spirit to you.

Paul now reminds the church of his previous instruction given during his visit to them (4:1-2). The first topic of "Christian distinctives" is holiness or wholeness. The Thessalonians stand out from the pagan culture in this instance by their sexual ethics.

The goal is sanctification; one way of reaching that goal is to renounce sexual immorality (4:3). The positive defense against immorality for the male believer is "to take a wife for himself in holiness and honor...." (4:4). This will distinguish the Christian from the heathens who, not knowing God, destroy each other "in the passion of lust" (4:5). Paul's ethical sanctions follow: God is our judge (4:6), He has called us to holiness (4:7), and the Holy Spirit has been given to empower a new life (4:8).

Paul addresses males in 4:4; they are to take a wife "in holiness and honor." The word translated "wife" literally means "vessel." It could be that each one is to take his own vessel or body in holiness rather than a wife. The word "vessel," however, is used in other literature to mean "wife" and this is probably Paul's intention.[1] If so, the Apostle sanctifies marriage as a part of God's will (4:3). A wife is to be taken not simply as a defense against immorality, but in holiness *and honor*. This is consistent with Paul's teaching elsewhere on the role and dignity of women in marriage (see Ephesians 5:21-33).

The Apostle is engaging in general exhortation here and thus only mentions men as taking wives. In I Corinthians 7:10ff, however, he speaks of the initiative responsibility of women in marriage.

Paul calls for the elevation of marriage above heathen corruption. Fidelity and honor between partners will make Christians stand out from their decadent surroundings and be a positive witness to their new life in Christ.

I Thessalonians 5:2-3

[2]For you yourselves know well that the day of the Lord will come like a thief in the night. [3]When people say, "There is peace and security," then sudden destruction will come upon them as travail comes upon a woman with child, and there will be no escape.

A further "Christian distinctive" is hope toward the future. This hope is grounded in the resurrection of Christ (4:14). Since He lives, we shall live, and those who have died will be raised by Him (4:16).

The glorious return of Christ, which is the consummation of Paul's hope, is called the "day of the Lord" (5:2). It is a day of resurrection, judgment, and the ultimate manifestation of God's kingdom and reign (see I Corinthians 15:20-28).

Paul teaches here that that day will come for unbelievers "like a thief in the night" (5:2). While they revel in false "peace and security," sudden judgment will fall upon them.

As a metaphor to express the suddenness of Christ's coming for the heathen, Paul employs not only the thief but also the travail of a pregnant woman (5:3). This is a traditional motif in apocalyptic thought. Travail expresses both surprise and pain. The resulting birth can also represent the new world which emerges from God's judgment (compare John 16:20-22). Paul, however, does not develop this thought here.

I TIMOTHY

Introduction

This "pastoral" letter is one of the few Pauline epistles directed to an individual. While Timothy, the Apostle's lieutenant, is its recipient (1:2), I Timothy also deals extensively with matters for the church in Ephesus (1:3) and Paul clearly has this larger context in mind.

In light of severe false teaching carried on by "certain persons" (1:3, 6), the Apostle calls Timothy and the church to hold to sound ("healthy") doctrine (1:10). The theological confusion includes "myths and endless genealogies" and speculations (1:4, 4:7) with a misapplication of the law (1:7). Those who desire to be "teachers of the law" fail to understand their own words and the substance of their instruction (1:7). Others are advocating the surrender of the responsibility of slaves to their masters (6:1-3). These persons are conceited, crave controversy and cause dissension (6:3-4). They also imagine that a godly life will bring material reward (6:5-10). Faith now becomes the means to their own selfishness.

Furthermore, not only is there internal confusion in the church, but some have departed from the faith, being deceived by false spirits and "doctrines of demons" (4:1). Their heresy includes asceticism, both in food and sex. Here we see a radical dualism in "what is falsely called knowledge" (6:20), which depreciates the body and this world for a hyper-spiritual life. Ethical chaos is the certain result (1:19).

Theological confusion is also producing disorder in the functioning of the church. For this reason Paul instructs Timothy with regard to the responsibilities of men, women (2:8-15), bishops (3:1-7; 5:17-22), deacons (3:8-9, 12-13), deaconesses (3:11), widows (5:3-16), and slaves (6:1-2).

In sum, I Timothy deals with the issues of church organization and ministry in a world of intellectual and moral confusion. As the church accepts its organizational needs, Timothy is to take a firm hand (1:3ff), remember Paul's witness (1:12-17), hold "faith and a good conscience" (1:19), and is to teach, order and correct the Ephesians. Barring Paul's return, I Timothy is written "so that, if I am delayed, you may know how one ought to behave in the household of God" (3:14-15). This letter gives us a context of theological and ecclesiastical responsibility in the face of chaos and confusion in which we can examine the role of women in the church.

I Timothy 2:8-10

[8]*I desire then that in every place the men should pray, lifting holy hands without anger or quarreling;* [9]*also that women should adorn themselves modestly and sensibly in seemly apparel, not with braided hair or gold or pearls or costly attire,* [10]*but by good deeds, as befits women who profess religion.*

Paul calls men to prayer (compare 2:1-4) and women to good deeds. For men this is contrasted with anger and quarreling (2:8). For women this is contrasted with the external adornment of costly fashions (2:9-10). Men are to evidence their faith in prayer. Women are to evidence their faith in action. Both of these calls contradict the problems in Ephesus which include strife (1:19-20; 6:3-5), and materialism (6:6-10).

While the admonition to prayer and good deeds may be in the context of the church's worship (2:1-2), the request for prayer "in every place" (2:8) suggests a more general setting. If this is so, the women's modest dress need not be simply to keep the men from lust during prayer. The women are to be always noted not for external style, but for acts of love. This is their lasting adornment: a change in life-style. To compete with each other in dress would only contribute to a worldly church and distracted attitudes among men (2:8). Here then is wise, practical exhortation.

I Timothy 2:11-15

[11]*Let a woman learn in silence with all submissiveness.* [12]*I permit no woman to teach or to have authority over men; she is to keep silent.* [13]*For Adam was formed first, then Eve;* [14]*and Adam was not deceived, but the woman was deceived and became a transgressor.* [15]*Yet woman will be saved through bearing children, if she continues in faith and love and holiness, with modesty.*

Paul now turns to the issues of women learning and teaching.[1] Some have desired to be teachers of the law and have wandered into vain discussion (1:6-7). Others engage in godless chatter and "contradictions of what is falsely called knowledge...." (6:20). While still others have departed from the faith altogether (4:1). Could some of those teaching falsely be women? Quite probably so.

Although women went uninstructed in the synagogue, they were immediately taught in the church. Gifted for ministry by the Spirit when incorporated into the body of Christ, some of these women easily achieved positions of authority. Those emerging from the synagogue, "desiring to be teachers of the law" (1:7), especially stood in the peril of abusing their new position and freedom. The lack of past instruction among Jewish-Christian women could account for some of the theological chaos in Ephesus.

In reaction to the abuse, undoubtedly some of the Jewish-Christian converts would have called for the women to be omitted from intruction altogether, as in the synagogue: "Give us the good old days." In opposition to this conservatism, Paul writes, "Let a woman learn...." (2:11). There is no going back to the old sexist exclusion.

At the same time, women are to receive instruction with silence and submissiveness (2:11). They must be taught before teaching. There must be no "myths and endless genealogies which promote speculations" (1:4) or "vain discussion" (1:6). This is the proper attitude for those receiving instruction.

As women are now taught, so they are not to engage in teaching. This they probably have prematurely done, adding to the disruption of the church (2:12). The phrase rendered "I permit no woman to teach or to have authority over men," appears to be timeless in English, that is, "I never ever allow a woman to teach...." However, in the Greek it is a present active indicative verb which can be translated "I am not presently permitting a woman to teach or to have authority over men...." Thus in contrast to the extremists demanding full women's liberation in Ephesus, Paul prohibits the teaching of those not properly instructed. But the verb tense cannot be made necessarily into a general principle for all time. The meaning of the infinitive "to have authority" is literally "to domineer." Women are neither presently to teach nor to rule over men. They are to learn in silence.

Paul continues, "For Adam was formed first, then Eve; and Adam was not deceived, but the woman...." (2:13-14). The ground for a woman's silence and submission appears to be her position in creation and deception. If this is the case, the word "for" is to be taken as the cause for silence. "For," however, may express nothing more than a continuation or connection as in I Timothy 2:5, "For there is one God and there is one mediator...."[2] If this is the case, "for" means "furthermore." Paul then would mean that women are to receive instruction from men not because Adam was formed first, but Adam's priority would merely be an analogy or illustration for the present situation of male priority in teaching.

If, however, "for" does express the ground for woman's silence and submission, then this is only a temporary situation as 2:13-15 clearly shows. While it is true that Adam has priority in creation and Eve priority in deception (2:13-14), this is erased in 2:15: "Yet woman will be saved through bearing children...." Unfortunately most translations fail to render the original language literally. It actually reads, "Yet she will be saved by the child-bearing (or the birth of the child)," namely, the Messiah. While Eve was deceived and became a transgressor, it is from her progeny that the child, that is, the Messiah has come (see Genesis 3:15). Thus as the Savior comes from a woman, she and all women are united corporately to Eve in redemption. Thus all women participate in bearing the Messiah. Their salvation, however, is not mechanical or material. They must continue "in faith and love and holiness, with modesty" (2:15). Both their inner disposition and outer life-style evidence their salvation.

One further point bears notice. Paul especially mentions Eve's deception and transgression (2:14). This is exactly the position of those who desire to be teachers of the law, but who use it "unlawfully" (1:7-8). This substantiates the probability that some false teaching is done by women. Also Paul's reference to Eve would satisfy the Jewish-Christian conservatives and appeal to Jewish-Christian women who now must only receive instruction.

Here, in conclusion, Paul's argument parallels I Corinthians 11:2-16. Women are to learn, not presently to teach or domineer over men. They are to be submissive and silent. Male priority is seen in Adam's creation and Eve's deception. While that deception may be illustrated in some of the theological confusion in Ephesus (1:6-7), redemption triumphs over the fall. A woman brings the Messiah to the world, and all women can experience salvation united to her (as "womankind"), but only as they persevere in faith, love, holiness and modesty. While Paul does not actually say it, we may rightly infer that the time will come for women to engage in the teaching task of the church once the abuses are corrected and they are properly instructed. Can she who bears the Messiah be prohibited from teaching His gospel?

I Timothy 3:1-2

[1]*The saying is sure: if anyone aspires to the office of bishop, he desires a noble task.* [2]*Now a bishop must be above reproach, the husband of one wife....*

The word "bishop" means "overseer." While singular, the word is used generically. Paul knows of "bishops" in the congregation, not of one ruling bishop (compare Philippians 1:1).

Among his qualifications, he must be the husband of one wife (3:2). While this could mean that he is not to be polygamous or adulterous, such sins need not be especially mentioned for bishops. They would hold true for all believers. Paul probably means that bishops are not to be divorced. This explains the emphasis in the original language on *one*.

With single marriages, bishops will be exemplary to their congregations, fulfilling God's intention in creation that marriage display "one flesh" (Genesis 2:24) and God's intention in redemption that marriage model the relationship between Christ and the church (Ephesians 5:21-33).

Note here the high value Paul places on marriage. As a bishop manages his family well, so he will manage the church well (see 3:4-5).

I Timothy 3:11

[11]*The women likewise must be serious, no slanderers, but temperate, faithful in all things.*

This word about women appears abruptly in the instruction about deacons (3:8-13). It is possible that it refers to the wives of deacons. If so, however, it is hard to explain why there is no similar exhortation to the wives of bishops above. It is improbable in the context that it applies to all the women in the congregation. Most likely, Paul addresses women deacons here. This would keep the verse from being an intrusion. Also in the original language there is no article "the" before women, as there is in English. Thus "women" is used adjectivally, "women who are deacons." There is no official title for them like "deaconesses" because the New Testament Greek does not assign a female gender to the word used for deacon.

Women deacons are to be serious, not engage in gossip ("no slanderers"), and be temperate and faithful. Along with men they must hold the faith and be morally pure (3:9).

Here is direct evidence for the inclusion of women in ministry "offices" in the church (compare Romans 16:1-2). This is also strong support for the interpretation of the injunction against women teaching in 2:11-15 as being temporary.

I Timothy 5:1-2

¹*Do not rebuke an older man but exhort him as you would a father; treat younger men like brothers, ²older women like mothers, younger women like sisters, in all purity.*

In the midst of exhortation to pastoral duties (4:11ff), Paul tells Timothy to relate to the members of the church after the model of the family.

Since God has called us into His family we are to live this out interpersonally. So older men are to be fathers; younger men are to be brothers (5:1). In parallel, older women are to be mothers; younger women are to be sisters (5:2).

Here is the nobility of the Christian community. Regardless of racial or social background, believers are now a family and are to be cared for by one another as one would care for his or her own flesh and blood. Honor and respect are due for the older, care and nurture for the younger. While sexual distinctions are maintained in the analogy, the value placed on each person could not be higher. The family tie is the deepest and most lasting.

I Timothy 5:3-8

³*Honor widows who are real widows. *⁴*If a widow has children or grandchildren, let them first learn their religious duty to their own family and make some return to their parents; for this is acceptable in the sight of God. *⁵*She who is a real widow, and is left all alone, has set her hope on God and continues in supplications and prayers night and day; *⁶*whereas she who is self-indulgent is dead even while she lives. *⁷*Command this, so that they may be without reproach. *⁸*If anyone does not provide for his relatives, and especially for his own family, he has disowned the faith and is worse than an unbeliever.*

One pressing problem in the early church was its responsibility for widows. When their husbands died, they had no immediate means of support. In dealing with this matter, Paul begins by reminding Timothy and the Ephesians of their call to honor widows (5:3). They must be real widows, however, who have been "left all alone" and trust only God for their care, continuing "in supplications and prayers night and day" (5:5). Thus these "real" widows are to be cared for by the church (see 5:9ff).

Widows who have children or grandchildren, however, must be cared for by their families (5:3-4). Reflecting the commandment to honor father and mother (Exodus 20:12), it is the families' duty to "make some return to their parents...." (5:4). Those children not providing for their parents are judged worse than unbelievers (5:8).

Up to this point then, Paul calls Christians to care for all widows and then distinguishes between those with family and those without. It is the families' task to care for the former group and not load this responsibility off on the church. It is the church's task to care for the latter group. The procedure to be followed is now expounded in 5:9-16.

I Timothy 5:9-16

[9]*Let a widow be enrolled if she is not less than sixty years of age, having been the wife of one husband;* [10]*and she must be well attested for her good deeds, as one who has brought up children, shown hospitality, washed the feet of the saints, relieved the afflicted and devoted herself to doing good in every way.* [11]*But refuse to enroll younger widows; for when they grow wanton against Christ they desire to marry,* [12]*and so they incur condemnation for having violated their first pledge.* [13]*Besides that, they learn to be idlers, gadding about from house to house, and not only idlers but gossips and busybodies, saying what they should not.* [14]*So I would have younger widows marry, bear children, rule their households, and give the enemy no occasion to revile us.* [15]*For some have already strayed after Satan.* [16]*If any believing woman has relatives who are widows, let her assist them; let the church not be burdened, so that it may assist those who are real widows.*

Paul now speaks of an "order" of widows who will be cared for by the church and have specific duties. There is to be a formal enrollment of those who qualify (5:9). The minimum age is sixty, which is the traditional point at which one becomes "old." Each widow must have been the wife of one husband (the ideal for a woman) and displayed her good deeds before the church and world (5:10). The catalogue that follows is suggestive, not exhaustive. Good deeds for a widow include raising her family, welcoming strangers, especially Christian missionaries ("shown hospitality''), washing the feet of the saints, evidencing both humility and hospitality (for Christ's example see John 13:3ff), caring for the afflicted and doing general good ''in every way.'' These ''pious acts'' which qualify widows for enrollment, are to be continued by their order in service to the congregation.

Excluded from the order are younger widows who will be tempted by their sexual desire to break from their association and remarry (5:11). Younger widows also will lack the Christian maturity and stability to devote themselves to prayer and good works because of their age and needs. Thus they ''learn to be idlers,'' ''gossips and busybodies'' (5:13). For this reason they need to remarry and have the responsibility of a household and children, not giving the Devil an occasion to stain the witness of the church as has already happened in some areas (5:14-15).

Paul concludes again that families have the primary financial responsibility for related widows and that the church should have to assist only those who are enrolled as ''real widows.''

From these verses the following points emerge. Firstly, the church accepted financial responsibility for those widows unable to care for themselves. Secondly, abuse of this among some widows made the ordering of this responsibility necessary. Thirdly, in light of the abuse, widows with families were to be supported by them, and younger widows were to be honest about their needs and not make pious commitments which they were unable to fulfill. Thus they should marry. (Generally speaking, the culture does not offer the economic option of a single life-style. At the same time, Paul does not hold that all women should automatically marry - compare I Corinthians 7:1ff). Fourthly, enrolled widows, supported by the church, are to engage in prayer (5:5) and works of mercy (5:10). Therefore, they share in the ministry of the church in acts of loving service and have a place of honor and dignity (5:3).

We see here Paul's response to a social issue with both generosity and care. A universal dole for widows is ruled out. Families are called to care for their own. Younger widows are not to deny their needs by making unkeepable commitments. Older women who are alone are to be bound together in ministry. Rather than a sense of hopelessness and uselessness, so characteristic of old-age, these widows are given new purpose and meaning as they serve the church in the name of Christ. Rather than being retired to obscurity and despair, they are called to a ministry along with the bishops and deacons of the church.

II TIMOTHY

Introduction

II Timothy has been called "the dying letter of the Apostle Paul." In it his ministry is entrusted to the next generation. Now facing certain death (4:6), Paul writes Timothy to exhort him in his service of Christ (4:1-5), and to equip him to build up the church. Thus the emphasis of the letter is that "what you have heard from me before many witnesses entrust to faithful men who will be able to teach others also" (2:2).

Paul begins by recalling warm memories of Timothy (1:3-7) and then asks him to share in his sufferings (1:8), remembering that Christ has conquered death (1:10).

Timothy is to deliver the gospel to others who will reproduce his ministry (2:1-2), centering himself in Christ (2:8). As a good teacher, he is to avoid "disputing about words" (2:14), "godless chatter" (2:16), "youthful passions" (2:22), "stupid, senseless controversies" (2:23), and those who have a form of religion but who deny its power (3:5).

As he teaches, Timothy is to remember Paul's example (3:10-13) and study the inspired scriptures (3:14-17).

After a call to fulfill his ministry (4:1-5), Paul gives his own witness as he faces death and requests that Timothy make a final visit to him (4:9). The letter ends with a shout of triumph: the Lord will keep Paul for his heavenly kingdom (4:18).

II Timothy 1:3-5

³*I thank God whom I serve with a clear conscience, as did my fathers, when I remember you constantly in my prayers. ⁴As I remember your tears, I long night and day to see you, that I may be filled with joy. ⁵I am reminded of your sincere faith, a faith that dwelt first in your grandmother Lois and your mother Eunice and now, I am sure, dwells in you.*

As Paul opens his letter the key word to take note of is *remember.* He prays for Timothy and warmheartedly recalls his tears, his faith, and his family of faith.

To begin with, Timothy is pictured as an emotional man— perhaps his tears were over Paul's departure. The memory of them kindles the Apostle's longing to see him again that he might be filled with joy (1:4).

Furthermore, Paul recalls Timothy's "sincere faith" and sees that faith dwelling first in his grandmother Lois and in his mother Eunice who was a believing Jewess (compare Acts 16:1). The sincerity of Timothy's faith is to be contrasted with those who only have a "form of religion" (3:5).

Paul singles out the two women who have been crucial in Timothy's life, and whose conversions paved the way for Timothy himself. The influence of Lois and Eunice for Christ is heralded here with clarity. Paul does not hesitate to mention them along with Timothy, and strongly imply the ministry which they had with him.

II Timothy 3:6-7

⁶*For among them [those living degenerately] are those who make their way into households and capture weak women, burdened with sins and swayed by various impulses, ⁷who will listen to anybody and can never arrive at a knowledge of the truth.*

In the immediate context, Paul warns that in the last days before Christ's return there will be a general moral collapse (3:1-5). This will be expressed in selfishness, materialism, attack upon authority, pleasure seeking, and a general breakdown in inter-personal relationships. While religion will be maintained as a form, the power of God will be denied (3:5). Timothy is to avoid people who live this way, using religion for selfish ends.

To illustrate, Paul speaks of those men who "capture weak women, burdened with sins and swayed by various impulses" (3:6). Here he parodies those false evangelists who make easy converts among foolish, uneducated women whose immoral lives respond to their immoral teachers. This depreciating caricature of women is designed to depreciate the false religionists who capture them.

They "make their way into households" because women would be less accessible to them in public. They evangelize "weak women" characterized by sin and moral and intellectual instability because this is their own state (see 3:1-5). Timothy is to stay clear of such people; they are a sign of the degenerate end times.

While Paul paints a demeaning picture of the "captured women" here, he paints an even more demeaning picture of the men who lead them into false religion and immoral lives (see 3:8-9). Nevertheless, he holds no demeaning view of women in general, both men and women share in the final corruption.

II Timothy 4:19

[19]*Greet Prisca and Aquila, and the household of Onesiphorus.*

Since Onesiphorus lived in Ephesus (1:16-18), we may assume that Prisca and Aquila are there. The greeting of his household may mean that he is deceased (see 1:18).

Notice that as in Romans 16:3 Paul names Prisca first (contrast I Corinthians 16:19). It is appropriate that the final words from Paul known to us contain greetings to this hearty couple who so loved him and labored with him. They are again singled out and honored.

II Timothy 4:21

[21]*Do your best to come before winter. Eubulus sends greetings to you, as do Pudens and Linus and Claudia and all the brethren.*

Paul asks Timothy to come before winter makes the sea impassible (compare 4:9). This is followed by greetings from unknown people who are probably leaders in the Roman Church. Among them one woman is mentioned, Claudia. Here again, women and men are joined in greeting and ministry without distinction.

TITUS

Introduction

Having concluded an extensive evangelistic effort with Titus on Crete, Paul now moves on to Nicopolis (3:12). Titus, however, remains and is instructed by Paul to organize the churches by appointing properly qualified elders in each town (1:5ff). At the same time he is to instruct his converts in sound doctrine (2:1), contending with the "circumcision party" (1:10).

This group appears to profess Christ but also engages in "Jewish myths" (1:24), being "empty talkers and deceivers" (1:10). Titus is to rebuke them (1:13), and teach by proper word and example (2:1, 7-8). If those who are factious do not repent, they are to be avoided.

Titus is to teach the churches concerning the responsibilities of older and younger men and women (2:1-6). Likewise he is to instruct slaves (2:2-10) and advocate submission to the state (3:1-2).

After contending for the truth of the gospel, and ordering the churches, Titus will then join Paul in Nicopolis (3:12).

Titus 1:5-6

⁵This is why I left you in Crete, that you might amend what was defective, and appoint elders in every town as I directed you, ⁶if any man is blameless, the husband of one wife, and his children are believers and not open to the charge of being profligate or insubordinate.

Paul begins his instruction to Titus by reminding him of his task to organize the churches by appointing elders. This is then followed by standards for eldership similar to those found in I Timothy 3:1-7.

In his guide for leadership, an elder (or "bishop," see 1:7) is to be morally blameless and have a believing family including responsible children. This is not only to insure his own faith but to set an example for his congregation (compare 2:7). Likewise, he is to be "the husband of one wife" (1:6). Here, as in I Timothy 3:2, the ideal of a single marriage is upheld. Behind this stands God's intention in creation that the two become "one flesh" (Genesis 2:24) in a permanent union.

Titus 2:3-5

[3]*Bid the older women likewise to be reverent in behavior, not to be slanderers or slaves to drink; they are to teach what is good,* [4]*and so train the young women to love their husbands and children,* [5]*to be sensible, chaste, domestic, kind, and submissive to their husbands, that the word of God may not be discredited.*

Older women have the responsibility of living their lives in such a way that younger women will learn from them how to live (2:3-4). They are to be "role-models" in the church for a godly life and thus pass on their faith to others.

Positively they are to be "reverent in behavior," that is, their outward expression is to evidence their inner devotion (2:3). Negatively, they are not to be gossips or enslaved to wine, two threats to any age, but especially older age.

"They are to teach what is good." The object of their teaching is to be "young women" (2:4). To restrict this teaching to example only, or domestic chores is both unnecessary and secularizing. Undoubtedly, the teaching of younger women embraces the whole of life. Paul focuses, however, on family duties: loving husbands and children. This includes being "sensible, chaste," namely faithful sexually, "domestic," caring for their household, "kind," especially to servants, and "submissive to their husbands." That this submission is out of love is clear from 2:4. Also from Ephesians 5:21ff it is submission to Christ's love given through their husbands to them. The goal of this training is "that the word of God may not be discredited" (2:5).

Paul gives helpful advice here to Titus. Older women have a divine calling to teach younger women. Younger women will learn the practical Christian life not from Titus but from older women. That life must be demonstrated to be understood. The training of younger women is designed to support a Christian home that will be exemplary. Obviously, this passage applies only to married younger women (2:4). The motive in all of this teaching is to honor the word of God (2:5).

PHILEMON

Introduction

The last and shortest letter in the Pauline corpus is one of the most attractive. In it the Apostle makes a personal appeal for Philemon, a past convert and church leader (see verses 1-2, 19), to receive back his runaway slave Onesimus (verses 15-16). Through unknown circumstances, Paul, while in prison, has become Onesimus' spiritual father (verse 10). Knowing of the slave's broken relationship with his master, Paul sends him home and writes this note to ensure his warm reception.

The letter to Philemon shows a master strategist at work facilitating reconciliation. For Paul, if redemption has really taken place, then it must be manifested in the slave owner and his slave being united as brothers in Christ.

Philemon 1-2

¹Paul, a prisoner for Christ Jesus, and Timothy our brother, to Philemon our beloved fellow worker ²and Apphia our sister and Archippus our fellow soldier, and the church in your house:

As Paul launches his appeal for Philemon to restore his runaway slave Onesimus, he identifies himself in humility as a "prisoner" and includes Timothy in his salutation.

Philemon is warmly greeted with a term of equality as "our beloved fellow worker" (compare Philippians 2:25, 4:3; Romans 16:3). Included with him are Apphia, Archippus and his house-church. As Philemon decides to welcome Onesimus back, he will have the encouragement (and pressure) of the Christian community.

"Apphia our sister" is presumably the wife of Philemon, being named immediately after him. If Archippus is his son, then Paul singles out the members of the household and follows by addressing the church.

Courtesy, tact, and the Apostle's relationship with Apphia motivate her being mentioned. It is also probable that she will share in the decision to welcome back Onesimus, since she would have authority over the household slaves.[1] Philemon does not stand alone. About him are a Christian wife, son, and the larger community for which and to which he is responsible (verses 4-7).

PART
THREE

CONCLUSION

CONCLUSION

What then does Paul teach about the role of women in the church? Is God's work in the world a "male show"? Do women tag along behind while men lead, speak, and battle for the faith? Are women to find their identity in dishes and diapers? What about male headship and female partnership? Is Paul contradictory, obscure, and confused, or does he bring the word of God to us in clarity and truth? Let us turn to our conclusions.

Woman's Place in God's Work

For Paul, women have an essential place in God's plan of salvation.

While Abraham is our father in the faith (Galatians 3:7), Sarah is our mother (Galatians 4:31). God's promise of a son to continue His saving purpose is given through her (Romans 9: 8-9). Living in that promise, she is the free woman who experiences and represents God's grace. Since the salvation promised to Abraham and Sarah is fulfilled in Christ, when we are united to Him by faith we are also united to Sarah's family from which He came. Here then is our human identity: sons and daughters of Sarah (Galatians 4:31).

Although Paul mentions other Old Testament women as continuing God's work, all climaxes in the fullness of time when God sent forth His Son, "born of a woman...." (Galatians 4:4). Jesus Christ enters the world through a human mother and the process of ordinary childbirth. What an enoblement of a basic female role and function. The Son of God could have come in some other way, but He didn't. He chose Mary to bear Him and for Paul all women share in that saving fact (I Timothy 2:15). Delight in motherhood! Mary was Jesus' mother! Delight in childbirth! Jesus was born of Mary! Eternity and time, God and man are united in Mary's womb.

Is redemption a "male show"? By no means! Place your faith in Christ and become a free child of Sarah our spiritual mother. Place your faith in Christ and remember that He was born of a woman. In the Pauline gospel then, womanhood is honored, blessed and exalted. God has and continues to do His work through women.

Women's Identity

Women as well as men are to find their lasting identity in Christ. Most of Paul's exhortation and teaching is addressed to both sexes indiscriminately. We are all to put on Christ (Romans 13:14), and to grow up into Christ (Ephesians 4:15). We are all gifted members of the body of Christ (I Corinthians 12:12). We are all being changed into the likeness of Christ (II Corinthians 3:18).

To claim that, for Paul, women are to find their identity elsewhere, either in domestic roles or in business success, is a perversion! Identity is not to be secured in this world. God has made us for Himself.

It is for this reason that Paul can endorse celibacy so heartily. Unmarried women are free from worldly troubles and can be anxious about the affairs of the Lord (I Corinthians 7:34). The Apostle's goal for married and unmarried alike is undivided devotion to the Lord (I Corinthians 7:35).

At the same time, Paul does not "iron out" created distinctions. Neither does he deny cultural sexual identity and roles. The Apostle has no abstract "platonic" ideal of humanity. His thought is historical and concrete and is controlled by the concrete historical Christ.

Within sexual and cultural identity Paul reflects both God's creation and his own age. Women play sexual roles of mother (Romans 9:9ff; II Timothy 1:5), grandmother (II Timothy 1:5), wives (I Corinthians 7:2ff; Ephesians 5:21ff; Colossians 3:18f; I Thessalonians 4:4; Titus 2:3ff), unmarried (I Corinthians 7:25ff), widows (I Corinthians 7:39; I Timothy 5:3ff), (by inference) children (Ephesians 6:1ff; Colossians 3:21), prostitutes (I Corinthians 6:15), and lesbians (Romans 1:26). No greater value is given to one role over another except where sexual deviation is attacked.

Because Christian women are called by Christ, however, they find new roles in Him which go beyond their traditional sexual and cultural ones. Thus they are sisters in the Lord (Philemon 2), helpers (Romans 16:2), deacons (Romans 16:1; I Timothy 3:11), fellow workers (Romans 16:3; Philippians 4:3), and even perhaps apostles (Romans 16:7, see our commentary above).

Modern writers too often picture Paul as seeing women finding their identity under the authority of men, veiled, silent and submissive. This is simply not true. Identity for all is in Christ. There is certainly nothing more and should be nothing less.

Paul's Use of Women's Identity

As we have seen, all Christians, male and female, are to identify with Sarah as their mother. Furthermore, Paul can view his own role with his new converts as "feminine." He loves them unconditionally and nurtures them like a nurse or mother holding her child against her breast (I Thessalonians 2:7-8). The Apostle is no chauvinist who excludes himself from identifying with female roles and tasks in order to protect his fragile male ego. On the contrary, he "nurses" the Thessalonians as a clear reflection of Christ's own extravagent love. Similarly, Christ would set us free today from sexual stereotyping so that the whole range of human experience might be used in communicating the truth of the gospel.

Women in God's Hierarchy

It is clear from Paul's letters that women are to function in a hierarchy of authority. This is expressed both in the headship of the male (I Corinthians 11:3; Ephesians 5:23) and in the subordination of the female (Ephesians 5:22; Colossians 3:18).

Commentators often base this hierarchy on God's created order as Paul himself writes that man is "the image and glory of God; but woman is the glory of man" (I Corinthians 11:7). Thus a secondary position for woman in Paul is assumed from the very beginning by many. This seems reinforced in I Timothy 2:14 where Paul states that woman was deceived before man. Thus, it is held, both from creation and the fall women are inferior. As one theologian writes, "...this headship of man is a divine absolute transcending the relativities of time and place,"[1] and, "The subordination of the woman to the man is an essential part of the hierarchy which God Himself has established to insure a proper order in the relationships of life."[2] Is this, however, the case?

Headship, as we have seen in our commentary, means life-source rather than lordship. Christ is the head of the church because He is its Savour who "loved the church and gave Himself up for her...." (Ephesians 5:25). As head He also nurtures her growth (Ephesians 4:15-16). This then must be the meaning for male headship: self-giving, nurturing love rather than autocratic rule.

At the same time, it is true that Christ is Lord of all creation, and that which stands in opposition to Him is under His feet (Ephesians 1:22; I Corinthians 15:25). This kingly reign, however, will end when all His enemies are defeated. As Paul proclaims,

"When all things are subjected to Him, then the Son Himself will also be subjected to Him who put all things under Him, that God may be everything to everyone" (I Corinthians 15:28).

Thus Christ's headship and lordship are not the essential structure of the way things are ("ontological"); they are the result of His triumph in salvation, in the re-creation of a new race, and in the defeat of God's enemies ("soteriological"). It is for this reason that we must take issue with those writers who see in Paul's hierarchical structure the necessary backbone of reality, an eternal law of nature which if violated will mean disorder and collapse for family and church.

Furthermore, because hierarchy now expresses Christ's saving work rather than the timeless structure of the universe, the submission of wives to their husband's headship is infused with a radically new content which most writers tend to overlook entirely or to underplay grossly.

The relationship between husbands and wives for Paul presupposes that both have first given themselves to each other in mutual submission as brothers and sisters in the Lord (Ephesians 5:21). Then husbands must express their mutual submission by loving their wives as Christ loved the church. This is the self-sacrificing, self-giving exercise of their headship (Ephesians 5:23-27).

In turn, wives are called to freely exercise their mutual submission in the Lord by subjecting themselve to the self-giving love of their husbands. It is Christ who determines both the mutual submission and its expression in the relationship between husbands and wives. Thus Paul exhorts, "Wives, be subject to your husbands, *as to the Lord,*" and "the husband is the head of the wife *as Christ is the head of the church,* His body, and is Himself its Savior" (Ephesians 5:22-23). For this reason the example of Christ and the work of Christ must take precedence over a submission formerly grounded in creation or the fall.

What we have seen then is that the hierarchical structure of relationships in Paul's writings is fundamentally based in Christ and His redemptive work. Both headship and submission exhibit aspects of that work. Christ's redemption is exhibited by male headship which gives itself. The church's response to redemption is exhibited in female submission. Since Christ came to serve and to give Himself, headship is servanthood. Rather than the subjugation of women under the male ego, women are now lifted to a new position as the hierarchy is infused with new content by Christ Himself.

That the position of women can be interpreted in an egalitarian manner is clear from passages such as Ephesians 2:6 where believers raised with Christ are seated *with* Him (sharing His rule) in the heavenly places and Romans 8:17 where we are "fellow heirs with Christ." This approach, however, misses the point because it focuses upon the male/female position rather than upon Christ Himself. If the person and work of Christ dominate our vision, then we will not be preoccupied with our position, rather we will be staggered by His grace which calls us all to reign with Him. Furthermore, He shows us that His reign is now exercised in sacrificial love which both male and female share, for example, when they give themselves to each other in marriage for the sake of Christ (Ephesians 5:21).

Thus we conclude that the hierarchical structure in Paul is dominated by Christ, is redemptive in its purpose, and is therefore revalued by His servanthood which can only liberate wives as they submit to the self-giving love of their husbands. Neither the male ego nor the female ego "win"; both are broken by Christ to express a life of surrender to Him, surrender to each other, and surrender to the world for which He died. Since hierarchy is revalued by *agape* love, this leads us naturally to see its expression in "partnership" without contradiction.

Women in Partnership

"Partnership," or better, "familyhood," is brothers and sisters in Christ, demonstrating the triumph of the gospel. This triumph will be examined in three contexts: theological, marital, and ministerial.

We begin theologically with the thesis text of Galatians 3:27-28, "For as many of you as were baptized into Christ have put on Christ. There is neither Jew nor Greek, there is neither slave nor free, there is neither male nor female; for you are all one in Christ Jesus." Krister Stendahl calls this verse a "breakthrough" in relation to the rest of Paul.[3] Paul Jewett describes it as the "Magna Carta of humanity."[4] Scanzoni and Hardesty assert, "Of all the passages concerning women in the New Testament, only Galatians 3:28 is in a doctrinal setting. The remainder are all concerned with practical matters."[5] Our view, however, is different.

We have seen that Paul views hierarchy as redemptive, headship as life giving, and husband and wife roles as based on mutual submission which is then acted out analogous to the relationship between Christ and the church. Therefore, rather than Galatians 3:28 being a "breakthrough" where "Rabbi" Paul dramatically becomes the Apostle Paul in one isolated moment of inspiration, what we now have is the unity and equality of the sexes expressed consistently with the rest of Paul's theology. Conflict, division, and discrimination are overcome in the hierarchy through mutual submission and servanthood which releases the love of Christ. Conflict, division, and discrimination are also overcome through the gospel which liberates Jews, Greeks, slaves, free men, and male and female from the bondage of the law and the limitations of the created order. Thus Paul writes that there is neither "male nor female" before God as all are equally baptized into Christ by faith. Now even the division of the sexes in creation (Genesis 1:27) is overcome. The ground of salvation is Christ's work and our faith alone, nothing else matters before God.

Moreover, Paul reaches the same conclusion in I Corinthians 11:2-16 where after endorsing female subordination in creation (woman being made from and for man and being the "glory of man"), he immediately shows that this is not the last word as he says, "nevertheless, in the Lord woman is not independent of man nor man of woman; for as woman was made from man, so man is now born of woman. And all things are from God" (I Corinthians 11:11-12). The key phrase is "in the Lord." In Christ the old divisions are transcended, and looking at creation through the gospel means that even in childbirth there is a sign for mutual dependency between the sexes as "man is now born of woman."

What we learn then from these texts is that the gospel triumphs. It is the last word. The unity and equality of the sexes stand on salvation by grace alone which makes us brothers and sisters in God's family. This does not, however, transcend sexual distinctions. Paul is not advocating a unisexual or homosexual model for the relationship between male and female. We are to live equally before God and with each other while recognizing our genital and cultural differences. In this respect the diversity of the sexes is sustained. Unity and equality in diversity, rather than "transcendence" (Scanzoni and Hardesty) is the result. Our diversity within male and female sexuality will be highly complex psychologically and culturally. Anatomy is not our destiny; Christ alone claims us and frees us to become what we are. Thus men may do yard work, auto repairs or dishes. Their identity is not established by their cultural roles which will vary. Their identity is established by Christ who creates and recreates them as brothers in God's family to live with sisters before the one Father.

If the theological basis for "partnership" or "familyhood" is found in the gospel of God's free grace to all, it is to be expressed in marital intimacy and ministerial service.

The equality of the sexes in marriage is expounded by Paul in I Corinthians 7. Throughout this chapter, as we have seen in our commentary, the Apostle deals with male and female responsibility symmetrically. For example, in the sexual intimacy between husbands and wives, "the wife does not rule over her own body, but the husband does; likewise, the husband does not rule over his own body, but the wife does." (I Corinthians 7:4). If we act out our identity in our sexuality, then Paul presupposes equality in the most sensitive area of human encounter. There is no hint of any "patriarchal" domination of the male. There is no suggestion that the male "owns" the female to do with her as he pleases. There is no suggestion that the wife must be a "Total Woman" catering to her husband's "special quirks, whether it be in salads, sex or sports,"[6] unless he in turn caters to hers. Each partner has equal rights and equal responsibilities. This is entirely consistent with the mutual submission of Ephesians 5:21 and husbands loving their wives with Christ's love while wives submit to this "in the Lord." The only result of this teaching will be mutual love, care and respect. As husbands and wives stand equally before Christ and share equally in sex, so they will live out their equality together in the expression of Christ in their marriage. The only inequality will be on the husband's part when he makes himself "below" his wife in serving her as Christ serves him. The Lord who loves him "descended" for his sake (Ephesians 4:9-10), renouncing His heavenly rights by emptying Himself, and taking the form of a slave (Philippians 2:5-7). This is the love the husband now extends to his submissive wife (Ephesians 5:25).

The theological basis for "familyhood" then is expressed both in the family and in the church. Since we are now all one in Christ Jesus, this must mean one in ministry. The gifts of the Holy Spirit are never given with preference to the male. We live in the church in the "new age" of redemption where the power of the Holy Spirit is shattering the old expectations and molds. Women are now exercising gifts of ministry by praying and prophesying (I Corinthians 11:5). Not only this, they are being "ordained" for ministry as well. Phoebe is a "deacon" and a "helper" (Romans 16:1-2). Prisca, Euodia and Syntyche are "fellow workers," standing side by side with men such as Aquila and Clement

(Romans 16:3; Philippians 4:2-3). The office of deacon is to be filled by women who are "serious, no slanderers, but temperate, faithful in all things" (I Timothy 3:11). Widows are to be enrolled for special ministry (I Timothy 5:3ff) and older women are to teach younger women their domestic duties (Titus 2:3-5).

The sharing of women in ministry calls forth the strongest affirmation from Paul. Phoebe has been a helper of the Apostle (Romans 16:2). Prisca joined Aquila in risking her neck for Paul and all the churches are thankful for her (Romans 16:3-4). Mary worked hard among the Romans (Romans 16:6). Rufus' mother mothered Paul (Romans 16:13). Nympha has a church in her house (Colossians 4:15). Chloe's people report to Paul (I Corinthians 1:11). Lois and Eunice have a sincere faith (II Timothy 1:5), and Apphia is a sister in the Lord to Paul and Timothy (Philemon 2). It is exactly the incidental nature of these references that makes them all the more impressive. Paul loved, affirmed, depended upon, and ministered with women. They in turn found a new identity and new roles both in Christ and in the Christian community. Catapulted beyond domesticity, women now carry out a full range of gifted functions, spreading the gospel and building up the church. Their veils, silence, and the prohibition against teaching men either maintained the formal structural expectations of the age, as in the case of veils, or was a temporary measure to correct abuse. It is only in the exercising of gifts that abuse is risked and discipline then necessary. The order of the church, however, must be determined not by creation or the fall but by Christ's work in redemption.

The gospel levels us, male and female, before God. We are all saved by faith alone. United to Christ, we reflect our new life of unity and equality in servanthood and familyhood. This is demonstrated in marriage and the church. Husbands serve their wives who are first sisters and then spouses. Wives submit to that service which elevates and enhances them. Men and women together use their gifts in building up the church and evangelizing the world. They are "fellow workers" in the gospel.

In Conclusion

Paul is consistent throughout his letters in bringing women into full equality with men based on the gospel. Thus he sees woman's crucial role in God's redemptive purpose through Israel's history which climaxes in the Incarnation. Women find their identity in union with Christ, not in marriage and the family. Thus Paul commends celibacy and marriage as vehicles for their discipleship.

Furthermore, Paul is free from sexual stereotypes and polarization. Both Christians and the Apostle can be given female identity.

By revaluing hierarchy, the Apostle brings this structural mode of thinking into the service of the gospel. Headship is servanthood. Submission is mutual. The object of female submission is the love of Christ through the male.

The relationship between hierarchy and partnership is found again in the gospel where all are one in Christ Jesus. Division is transcended while distinctions are maintained. Unity in Christ is dynamic and enriching, not monotonous and bland. This oneness in Christ is demonstrated in marriage and ministry. Female sexual responsibility is equal to men. Female ministerial responsibility is equal to men, "for all are one in Christ Jesus." What then does our study have to say to the church and to the world?

To The Church

The church must divest itself as a whole from male presumption which discriminates against women in the use of their gifts and in creating opportunities for ministry. For far too long the church has been controlled and dominated by men. Again and again Paul has been called in to support women's inferior status and position. When the Pope announces that "If the role of Christ were not taken by a man...it would be difficult to see in the minister the image of Christ,''[7] he confuses Christ's image with male identity, overlooking entirely that both men and women are to be conformed to the one Lord (II Corinthians 3:18).

The barring of women from the pulpit, the seminary lecture hall, and the pastor's office only weakens the church, denying the full use of the spiritual gifts of half its members. This must stop! Where women, under the lordship of Christ, have been free to use their gifts great blessing has followed. One contemporary example is Henrietta C. Mears who was Director of Christian Education at the First Presbyterian Church of Hollywood, California, for over 30 years. In that time she taught the college Sunday School class of over 500 members weekly, ran the whole Sunday School of over 6,000 members, saw literally hundreds of men and women called into full time Christian vocations, founded Gospel Light Press which provides Sunday School Curriculum to over 20,000 churches, founded Forest Home Christian Conference Center where over 35,000 people attend retreats annually, and was the guiding light for Bill Bright in his starting Campus Crusade for Christ. Women silent in the church? Women never teaching men? Both Paul's letters studied in their context and Christian history show that these conclusions are humbug!

Where are the women deacons fulfilling ministerial tasks? They functioned in Paul's churches; why do they not function in ours? The answer: because we are not Biblical churches. Where are women leading in prayer and prophecy in our congregations? They were in Paul's churches; why do they not function in ours? Again, the answer is because we are not Biblical churches.

But someone replies, "Ordination is different." Jesus called only male apostles (Did He? See Romans 16:7 in the commentary above) and Paul speaks only of male elders. Leadership then must be in the hands of men. While the data is accurate, the conclusion is not. "Ordination" as we understand it today is far different from the early church where there was no clergy-laity distinction. There was only a distinction in gifts, and since women as well as men were and are gifted for ministry, they must be allowed to use their gifts.

Certainly in the religious and historical context it was necessary for the Twelve Apostles to be men since, among other things, they represented the twelve sons of Jacob and thus the 12 tribes of Israel reconstituted by the call of Christ. Women apostles would have confused the imagery of the church as the new Israel. At the same time, as we have seen, women functioned formally and informally in ministry because they were called by Christ and gifted by the Holy Spirit. The church can only accept and affirm Christ's gifts, it cannot fabricate them. When this is done in a sexist way the New Testament theology and practice is abandoned for cultural presumption against women. More devastatingly, the gospel is compromised if not denied because Christ's redemption which makes us one is contradicted by our practice. The result is a mocking world and a weakened church. Rather than finding true female identity and liberation in Christ, the world is forced to view Christ and the church as the subjectors of women. The world then creates political and economic gospels which only emancipate to enslave, becoming themselves idolatrous. Now women are liberated by becoming men (unisex) or by abandoning men (political lesbianism). What absurdity - this is a judgment upon the failure of the church.

Women will only be liberated as the church is used by God to bring them to new life in Christ in the context of a redemptive community where they experience a choice of roles consistent with their calling and gifts. For some this may be entirely domestic. For others there may be little that is traditional. All will be welcomed and loved by Christ and be used to build and strengthen His body, the church. Rather than becoming "Fascinating Women" by playing to male weakness from a position of power, they will be modelling their lives after Christ in mutual submission to men. Rather than becoming the "Total Woman" by catering to the male, they will become "Total Christians" as they reach their spiritual potential in Christ together with men. Rather than living under a male hierarchy which defines them as inferior and needing protection, they will discover that hierarchy as service and they will be liberated by the Christ who loves them through it. Rather than seeking to deny their distinctiveness in some abstraction of "transcendence," they will rejoice in their uniqueness and discover how created differences enrich their equal ministry in the body of Christ. Rather than embracing "partnership" in distinction to "hierarchy," they will discover how hierarchy serves them within the one family of Christ.

We must not lose the point. The strength, growth and life of the church in our generation is dependent upon our openness to welcome women fully into Christian ministry. To fail here will be a denial of the gospel of reconciliation. To fail here will mean an elimination of massive gifts given to strengthen the church through women. To fail here will be a contradiction to the gospel we proclaim and demonstrate to the world.

To The World

The church of Jesus Christ is to be that redeemed community of believers showing the world that the gospel is true by its lifestyle, as well as by its message.

The world struggles for liberation. Women seek identity beyond stereotyped roles, pseudo-revelations of "anatomy is destiny," and vicarious living through husbands and children. Where is their authentic identity to be found? The answer is in a personal relationship with Jesus Christ. We can live only when our sins are forgiven, when we are "born again" into new life in Christ, when God's Holy Spirit indwells us. This transpires, not by mental assent or positive thinking, but by turning from our old life and embracing Christ by faith. Now we know who we are: children of God. Our identity is secure, not in family, church or worldly vocation. Our identity is secure in Christ.

The shattering insights of Betty Friedan's "feminine mystique" results in a longing for growth, "personhood," meaning and self-worth. But where is this to be found? The church must answer by word and lifestyle - in Christ and in Christ alone.

The truth of "transcendence" is that both male and female stand before God and each other equal in sin and salvation. The falsehood of "transcendence" is that it denies created distinctions for living in this world. Truth is not to be found in the denial of our creaturehood as male and female, nor is it to be found in homosexuality. Truth is to be found in Christ and His call. This may well lead to celibacy or marriage, vocational ministry or lay ministry. Christ promises to guide our lives and fulfill us whether behind a sink of dirty dishes or a pulpit. When He is our life, when He is our passion, when He is our fulfillment, then all else will fall into place. We are called to live "extra nos," outside of ourselves (Luther). Thus we will not live preoccupied with our place or our rights. We will live preoccupied with Him as He judges our selfishness and our jockeying for position in the church and in the world. This means, however, that we cannot withdraw into pseudo-spirituality and avoid the longing and the cry of women today. Liberated by Christ we live "extra nos" toward our Lord and toward others. We must not rest until all women are liberated to become what Christ calls them to be - to be conformed to Him. We therefore must denounce the false liberationist gospels, while affirming the longing expressed in them. At the same time, we must expose and attack the dehumanizing of women in our culture sexually, vocationally and economically, whenever this takes place. But our calling is yet more intense than this. We must call all women (and men) to Christ as their only liberation and only hope, and we must demonstrate to the world in the body of Christ that we mean what we say.

Christ brings a new identity to women. Paul stands, not as an obstruction, but as a herald of that identity. The gospel of Christ has created it. The church of Christ must embody it. Together as men and women we look to the future when Christ will consummate His redemption and our unity in His triumphant return. Until then we struggle through with our sin and pride undercutting us and the grace and presence of Christ transforming us, and we lift up our heads for our redemption draweth nigh.

Our call in the world is to Christ. We are to be a colony of heaven. In this world neither men nor women will be fully equal, for sin will continue to distort and corrupt us. Yet something new has happened. Jesus has come and He makes all things new. As we live under His lordship more and more, the world will see that all are one in Christ Jesus.

The world watches. The church struggles. Christ's call is clear. The question now is not whether we know it. The question is whether we will do it. Let us go forward together unto the Lord that we may be whole and that the world may believe.

INTRODUCTION

1. *Time magazine*, February 7, 1977, p. 65.

PART I - A SURVEY OF CONTEMPORARY VIEWS

1. These authors are a representative sample of a growing body of literature. Especially recommended is also Richard and Joyce Boldrey, *Chauvinist or Feminist? Paul's View of Women* (Grand Rapids: Baker Book House, 1976).
2. Helen Andelin, *Fascinating Womanhood* (Santa Barbara, Ca.: Pacific Press, 1965), p. 57.
3. *Ibid.*, p. 90.
4. *Ibid.*, p. 109.
5. *Ibid.*, p. 117.
6. *Ibid.*, p. 144.
7. *Ibid.*, p. 163.
8. *Ibid.*, p. 165.
9. *Ibid.*, p. 169.
10. *Ibid.*, p. 89.
11. Marabel Morgan, *The Total Woman* (N.Y.: Pockets Books, 1975), p. 19.
12. *Ibid.*, pp. 20-21.
13. *Ibid.*, p. 26.
14. *Ibid.*, p. 34.
15. *Ibid.*, pp. 38, 42.
16. *Ibid.*, p. 52.
17. *Ibid.*, p. 60.
18. *Ibid.*, p. 63.
19. *Ibid.*, p. 76.
20. *Ibid.*, p. 82.
21. *Ibid.*, p. 83.
22. *Ibid.*, pp. 84-85.
23. *Ibid.*, pp. 96-97.
24. *Ibid.*, p. 130.
25. *Ibid.*, p. 238.
26. *Ibid.*, p. 244.
27. *Ibid*
27. *Ibid.*
28. *Ibid.*
29. Larry Christenson, *The Christian Family* (Minneapolis: Bethany Fellowship, 1970), p. 14.

30. *Ibid.*, p. 6.
31. *Ibid.*, p. 17.
32. *Ibid.*, p. 18.
33. *Ibid.*
34. *Ibid.*
35. *Ibid.*, p. 32.
36. *Ibid.*, p. 35.
37. *Ibid.*, p. 44.
38. *Ibid.*, p. 47.
39. *Ibid.*, p. 54.
40. *Ibid.*, p. 127.
41. *Ibid.*, pp. 127-128.
42. *Ibid.*, p. 135.
43. *Ibid.*, p. 39.
44. Betty Friedan, *The Feminine Mystique* (N.Y.: Dell Publishing Co., 1974), p. 37.
45. *Ibid.*, p. 53.
46. *Ibid.*, p. 96.
47. *Ibid.*
48. *Ibid.*, p. 115
48. *Ibid.*, p. 115.
49. *Ibid.*, p. 69.
50. *Ibid.*, p. 149.
51. *Ibid.*, p. 163.
52. *Ibid.*, p. 197.
53. *Ibid.*, p. 218.
54. *Ibid.*, p. 250.
55. *Ibid.*, p. 269.
56. *Ibid.*, p. 332.
57. *Ibid.*, p. 4.
58. *Ibid.*, p. 79.
59. Letha Scanzoni and Nancy Hardesty, *All We're Meant to Be* (Waco, Texas: Word, 1974), p. 15.
60. *Ibid.*, p. 21.
61. *Ibid.*, p. 22.
62. *Ibid.*, p. 28.
63. *Ibid.*, p. 29.
64. *Ibid.*, p. 31.
65. *Ibid.*, p. 67.
66. *Ibid.*, p. 69.
67. *Ibid.*
68. *Ibid.*, p. 71.

69. *Ibid.*
70. *Ibid.*, p. 76.
71. *Ibid.*, p. 84.
72. *Ibid.*
73. *Ibid.*, p. 104.
74. *Ibid.*, pp. 106-107.
75. *Ibid.*, p. 107.
76. *Ibid.*, p. 112.
77. *Ibid.*, p. 118.
78. *Ibid.*, p. 136.
79. *Ibid.*, p. 144.
80. *Ibid.*, p. 157.
81. *Ibid.*, p. 181.
82. *Ibid.*, p. 184.
83. *Ibid.*, p. 185.
84. *Ibid.*, p. 201.
85. *Ibid.*, p. 208.
86. Paul Jewett, *Man as Male and Female* (Grand Rapids: Eerdmans, 1975), pp. 13-14.
87. *Ibid.*, p. 49.
88. *Ibid.*
89. *Ibid.*, p. 14.
90. *Ibid.*
91. *Ibid.*, p. 51.
92. *Ibid.*
93. *Ibid.*, pp. 51ff.
94. *Ibid.*, p. 57.
95. *Ibid.*, p. 71.
96. *Ibid.*, p. 85.
97. *Ibid.*, p. 142.
98. *Ibid.*, p. 148.
99. *Ibid.*, p. 130.
100. Excepting II Thessalonians which has no reference to women. The Pastorals are here accepted as Pauline.

PART II - THE PAULINE EPISTLES

Romans

1. Cited in Jewett, *op.cit.*, p. 91.
2. Cited in William Sandy and Arthur Headlan, *The Epistle to the Romans* (Edinburgh: T.&T. Clark, 1902), p. 423.

I Corinthians

1. See Hans Conzelmann, *I Corinthians* (Philadelphia: Fortress Press, 1975), pp. 135-136.

2. For the evidence see *Ibid.*, pp. 184-186.

3. Cited in Leon Morris, *The First Epistle of Paul to the Corinthians* (Grand Rapids: Eerdmans, 1958), p. 154.

4. See Herman Ridderbos, *Paul, An Outline of His Theology* (Grand Rapids: Eerdmans, 1975), p. 382 and Marcus Barth, *Ephesians 1-3* (Garden City, N.Y.: Doubleday, 1974), pp. 183ff.

5. See James Moffatt, *The First Epistle of Paul to the Corinthians* (London: Hodder and Stoughton, 1938), p. 151.

6. That Paul reflects Jewish discussion and exegesis here is not to be doubted. See Conzelmann, *op. cit.*, p. 186. Paul's argument rests, however, on Genesis, not Jewish speculation.

7. Note that this independent dignity as created in the image of God is established prior to their sexual union. Moreover, the image of God is only reflected totally in *both* male and female. This happens neither in their alienation from each other (homosexuality) nor in their assimilation to each other (unisexuality).

8. H. Chadwick in "All Things to All Men," *New Testament Studies*, Vol. I. (1954-55), pp. 261ff., takes another approach, holding that here Paul grants his opponents' position and then moves them to his own. We hold, however, that Paul accepts the old orders and then pours new content into them.

"That is why a woman ought to have a veil (authority) on her head, because of the angels." This obscure verse has been explained as referring either to fallen angels (demons) who would be evilly attracted to an unveiled woman or good angels who protect the proper order of worship, and must not be offended. The latter makes the most sense, especially as the whole context is that of worship. The angels upholding a particular cultural order should not make that order into a timeless necessity. That angels defend order, however, is always true.

9. H. Conzelmann, *op. cit.*, p. 246.

10. Krister Stendahl, *The Bible and the Role of Women* (Philadelphia: Fortress Press, 1966), p. 30.

II Corinthians

1. The issue of the unity of II Corinthians does not concern us here.

Galatians

1. See Stendahl, *op. cit.*, p. 32.

Ephesians

1. The R.S.V. "respect" is "fear" in Greek. This is employed not because husbands are to keep their wives in fearful subjection, but because of the Christological context. As husbands love their wives with Christ's love, so wives respond with godly fear as the church "fears" Christ (i.e. is aweful in worship before Him). See Marcus Barth, *Ephesians 4-6* (Garden City, N.Y.; Doubleday, 1975), pp. 648ff.

I Thessalonians

1. See Walter Bauer, *A Greek-English Lexicon of the New Testament* (Chicago: University of Chicago Press, 1957), p. 761f.

I Timothy

1. For what follows I am partially indebted to Dr. Philip Payne.
2. See Bauer, *op. cit.*, p. 151.

Philemon

1. See Eduard Lohse, *Colossians and Philemon* (Philadelphia: Fortress Press, 1971), p. 190.

PART III - CONCLUSION

1. Jewett, *op. cit.*, p. 51
2. *Ibid.*, p. 57.
3. Stendahl, *op. cit.*, p. 32.
4. Jewett, *op. cit.*, p. 142.
5. Scanzoni and Hardesty, *op. cit.*, p. 71.
6. Morgan, *op. cit.*, p. 60.
7. *Newsweek Magazine*, Feb. 7., 1977, p. 77.